UNGUARDED
Heart

Amelia McTaggart

Unless otherwise indicated, all scriptures are from the *American King James Version* (AKJV) and are used by permission.

ISBN: 978-1-944566-18-0
Copyright © 2016 by Amelia McTaggart

All rights reserved. No part of this publication may be reproduced, stored in a retrieval system, or transmitted in any form or by any means without the prior written permission of the author or publisher.

In loving memory of Sabrina Marie Schirn,

Sabrina, the memories you left and the impact that you had on my heart are something that I cherish and did from the very start. I remember when I asked God to please never let our friendship part. I asked for Him to let us forever be friends. As everyone knows, true friendship never ends. But now I understand, with death, true life just begins. Rest in peace and reside in the heavens, dear Bri.

Love,
Your friend, Milz

Aunt Dawn, you may have never known just how amazing you were, but I can say that God used you so I could have my freedom back. For once, the saying you used to always say, "Honey, we just have to leave it to God," was truly what made my life story.

Rest in peace now and forever,
Love,
Your niece, Amelia

Foreword

I believe most mothers, no matter what kind of relationship we have or have had with our daughters, want the best for them. We most certainly want them to be safe. Above all, we want them in abuse free relationships, especially if abuse is not a common or everyday event in one's household. I was no different and our home rarely heard a raised voice, much less any sort of abuse, physical or otherwise. How it came to be that my own daughter became a victim of physical, emotional and sexual abuse has baffled me. But I can vouch for this, once the cycle starts, it self generates and gains momentum, drawing the victim into a spiral that literally sucks them inside. Most victims can find no way out of what can become a "living hell."

I don't believe, we as parents of abused daughters, ever really know the true extent of the abuse that the victim "covers" for her perpetrators. How quickly the abuse escalates into extreme violence is, at best, mind-boggling. My husband and I tried everything from tough love, to many a night on our knees crying out to God to save our daughter, pleading with Him to rescue her from this madness. Nothing seemed to help. There seemed to be no answer, no resolve. Nothing.

I had received phone calls in the middle of the night from our daughter to come pick her up from places I did not know even existed. I certainly knew they were dark, dangerous places that young girls should never visit. I saw bruises and evidence of violent beatings that she refused to report. We saw her continue to protect, even go to jail for her abusers. Even more alarming was her return to the abusers, over and over again. Nothing seemed able to stop the cycle. All we could do was pray that she somehow survived and that her abuser did not ultimately take her life. Then later we had to pray that he would not kill her children as well. We knew he was abusing them all.

We tried talking to her, but she was not there. Her eyes were vacant pools, nothing sunk in. I could not seem to pierce the veil that she was hiding behind. But God, who is faithful, who has promised…in the midst of the darkest storm… made a way. What is so amazing and miraculous is not only the absolute miracle of her escape and survival, but the supernatural and miraculous transformation that took place in her in such a short period of time.

After years and years of never having, what I would call, a "normal" conversation, she has become a caring and protective mother to her two children, and an amazing advocate for abused women. For those that have yet to escape the violence and vicious cycle of abuse, the answer, a clear shot to freedom awaits you.

This book is dedicated and exists to be an answer and a simple guide to God's doorway out for others who find themselves in this trap and need a way of ESCAPE.

—Debra McTaggart

Chapter One

"Don't be ashamed of your story, it just may inspire someone."
—Toby Mac

I grew up in a loving Christian home. For as long as I can remember, which is sometime around three years of age, I knew that I always wanted a family of my own, just like the one I had growing up. I desired a loving husband, great kids and most importantly for God to be the head of my household. My dreams, however, were shredded and my heart torn apart at a most vulnerable time in my life. At the age of three, I was molested by one of my Christian schoolteachers. I was haunted by nightmares as I relived it night after night. As a young child, I did not understand why I felt the way I did. By the time I was four I was having explicit sexual thoughts no child should ever have. I never understood what was wrong with me. However, God got me through those younger years and did not let it destroy my joy.

Then at the age of ten, tragedy hit my family. My father had a stroke. I always had a wonderfully close relationship with my father. I was "daddy's little girl." My father was an inventor, a well-accomplished man who gave us everything we ever needed and much of what we wanted, but the stroke had left him with mood swings and one side of his body numb. My father was a godly man and difficult to anger, but the stroke left many changes in him. One day he announced that he wanted to go back to the island where he grew up. At the time my parents did not tell the three of us kids why it was necessary to move. I guess, considering we were children, they did not feel we could handle the truth. However, my father believed he was going to die. He had heard that most people suffer strokes again after you have one and that the second or third one normally kills you. So we packed up our belongings and moved to the island. No one could have imagined what events would soon take place in my life.

I began going to a Christian school on the island. I started making friends and living as normal a life as any girl my age could live. Then, a week shy of my thirteenth birthday, a Category 5 hurricane hit, leaving the entire island without power. It left many people without food or water. Many families, including my own, were forced to evacuate and flee to the States.

Before I go any further with my story, allow me to go back one year before the hurricane. I had become friends with an eighth grade girl named Evi. I was a year behind her in school. Like most eighth graders, she was really into boys. She introduced me to a lot of different guys, who were older than me. However, I took a particular interest in one boy in her class. His name was Frankie and we became close friends. While I was in Florida, after the hurricane, Frankie and I talked on the phone all the time. I had other boyfriends, but nothing serious. While I was living back in the States I became depressed. I felt so alone and I really missed my friends on the island.

After two months in the States, I received a call from Evi who she told me her mother had passed away. I wanted to be there for Evi during this difficult time because I was her best friend. We did literally everything together. I felt compelled to be with her during this tough time. She was back on the island and she let me know the power was up in some places. She said our school was being run out of a church. After some time of begging my parents to let me go, they gave into my wishes. So my dad and I flew down to the island. He was going to get everything ready for my mom, brother and sister to come down as soon as they were able.

The next week I began going back to my school, which was temporarily in a church. I was more than happy to see all of my friends. I spent most of my time at Evi's house just trying to offer her support. I wanted to be there for her. It wasn't long before Frankie and I began developing feelings for each other, strong feelings. I had boyfriends before, but I never really fell in love. My dad was never at our new home. He was trying to get things together for my mom and siblings to come down. So I would often invite Evi over. One day Evi told me a secret she had been keeping. She told me that she had lost her virginity. She began saying how cool she thought it was. Evi was only fourteen years old. Needless to say, I was in shock! Sex had never entered my mind yet. I mean I had starting doing things most thirteen year olds probably shouldn't do, but on the island making out with guys and letting them "feel you up" was normal at that age.

Evi told me that I should have sex too. She felt it would help us relate to each other more. She kept telling me how it was so much fun. Evi and Frankie were neighbors and were close friends. I was totally head over heels for Frankie.

One day Evi told me, "You should lose it to Frankie. I mean you guys are in puppy love, aren't you?" Even though neither one of us ever told the other one that we loved each other, I believed he loved me as much as I loved him. I just felt really close to him. One day when I knew my dad was going to be out of the house for a long time and had a lot of things to do, I told Evi to come over. She was talking to Frankie's best friend, Johnny, so we invited both of them over. We all "chilled out" by watching a movie on the couch. When the movie was over we went in to my bedroom.

I had two bedrooms, but we were all lying on my bed and then Evi was telling a story about these girls and boys and how they were going to have sex. Evi would always tell stories to liven things up. Unfortunately, pressure began to build. I was getting so nervous I felt like I was going to throw up. Then Frankie grabbed my hand and led me into my other bedroom. I was so scared as he started kissing me. He laid me down on the bed. My heart began racing when he got on top of me. I remember being very bashful and just looking at the corner of the ceiling in my room. It hurt a lot more than what Evi said it would. The deed was done as I gave myself to Frankie that day. Frankie was my first and, at the time, I thought we would be together forever. I often prayed, "Oh God, let him be with me forever. I love him so much."

Two days after I had sex I went back to school and saw Frankie, but this time he acted differently. I stopped him in the hall and asked him, "What's wrong?"

He looked down at the ground and then back at me, "I think we should just be friends. I like another girl now." When Frankie said that my heart sank and for the first time in my young life I felt my heart break. Little did I know then it was only the beginning of many more heartbreaks to come.

The next day a second grader asked me, "Did you really have sex with Frankie?" I was so embarrassed. Evidently Frankie had told Ryan and Ryan told someone else who told a whole bunch of people. Practically the whole school knew by now. I hated going to school after that. To make matters even worse, Evi stopped talking to me. I felt used and alienated. My self-esteem and self-worth were destroyed. I spiraled into a state of depression that led to me cutting myself. I thought it would relieve the pain of what I was feeling inside. I became addicted to sex, not caring about feelings or the person, just sex. Most of the guys I started having sex with had girlfriends and they did not care about me in the least bit. I could not blame them, however, because I did not care about them either. I told myself I was going to use guys before they used me again. For some reason that was the only way I felt in control, not catching feelings for anyone. By the time I was fourteen I was into drugs, sex and alcohol. I had totally forgotten about God and liked the feeling of staying numb to life. I mean I would talk to God now and then, but honestly, I was angry with Him. About a year later Frankie apologized to me, but too much damage had already been already done.

Shortly after Frankie apologized Evi and I began talking with each other. She asked me to go to a party with her on the beach. I was still fourteen at the time. Evi and her other friend, Shawni, came over to my house to get ready. After we got dressed and made up, we headed to the party. We were walking past the bathroom stalls when some guy grabbed my hand and began saying how beautiful I was. I had never seen the guy before, but I always enjoyed compliments and, quite frankly, he was quite good looking. He asked if we could get away from the noise and the crowd and talk privately. He told me his name was Robbie. We began walking along the beach and he reached for my hand. It seemed harmless to me. Then suddenly we reached a slope on the beach where you could not see what was going on by the water. He stopped and dropped to a sitting position, still holding my hand, which automatically made me lose my balance. I was very short and smaller than Robbie. He started kissing me, but something in me felt uneasy, something was just not right. I felt like this was moving way too fast. For the first time, since I had lost my virginity, I did not want to have sex. A feeling of sheer terror came over me.

I stopped him from kissing me and said, "Hey, lets go back to the party."

His entire facial expression changed. He became angry. He shouted, "No! I am going to have sex with you."

The minute I heard that I tried to jump up as fast as I could. He grabbed me, jerked me to the ground and climbed on top of me. I felt his hand moving my skirt. I squirmed and struggled to get him off as I started screaming.

He quickly put his hand over my nose and mouth and whispered in an angry voice, "I will kill you by cutting off your air if you keep screaming." I was raped right then and there. I could not grasp the reality of it. I felt dirty and disheveled.

After he finished with me and rolled off he whispered, "I'm sorry." I ran as fast as I could back towards the party. My entire body was aching. I ran up to Evi, who was sitting under some trees and said in a whimpering voice, "I was just raped." She was with some of our close guy friends. They all jumped up in anger and went running on the beach to find him, but Robbie was nowhere to be found. People said they had seen him running very quickly across the beach, but no one thought anything of it.

After the night I was raped I was angrier than ever with God and totally distanced myself from Him. Two months later I was out at the movies with my friends. For the first time since the rape Robbie appeared. My whole body shook and I was as scared as I was the night it happened.

I called one of my close friend's, Miles, who was older. I whispered, "He is out here. That guy, Robbie is here."

Miles was across the parking lot at a club, so he said, "Walk over here. We are going to deal with this here and now." I met Miles and we walked over to Robbie.

A crowd surrounded us and my heart began beating harder and faster. We were in a dark, empty field that people used as a path to get from the movies to a fast food restaurant. A lot of older guys would hang out there in their cars, smoke "weed" and drink. Normally, they would hit on any young girl that walked across. As we approached Robbie, Miles put me in front of him. I was five feet and Miles was six feet tall so he talked over top of me.

One of Robbie's friends asked, "What happened?"

Miles said, "I want to ask your boy something." I had no desire to even look in Robbie's eyes. I had not been able to look in any guy's eyes while having sex since the rape.

All of a sudden Robbie broke the silence and said, "What is the problem?"

Miles got up in his face and answered, "I know what you did to her and if you ever get near her or even breathe hard near her again you and I are going to have problems." Then Miles backed up to see what Robbie had to say.

Robbie then screamed out, "So what if I raped her what are you going to do about it?"

I was still in front of Miles as the argument began getting very intense. Suddenly, I felt someone pull me very hard to the side out of Miles' way. It looked like Robbie had punched Miles in the stomach, but it was not a punch. Miles looked at his shirt and then Robbie started running away. Miles went running after him towards the movies. I began running after Miles when I saw a large, bloody kitchen knife on the ground. I was in shock. Miles had been stabbed! I ran as fast as I could to Miles who was near the movie theater by now. As I approached him, I could see his white shirt was full of blood and he was sweating profusely. I hugged him tightly, told him how much I loved him and it that it was going to be ok. I could not stop crying as I dialed 911 and reported that my friend had been stabbed.

Miles was rushed to the hospital and for the first time since I had been raped, I prayed. "God, please do not let my friend die. Please!" At the hospital they told us he was in emergency surgery. Miles survived the stabbing and I was overjoyed.

Two months after that, I met a boy named Cray at a party. His friend, Dale, was trying to hit on me. However, my friend, Amy, said that he was her ex-boyfriend and she was still madly in love with him. So, I kept talking to Cray. We began dating and it wasn't long before we were head over heels for each other.

The wonderful feelings didn't last long, however. About two months after we began dating we started having arguments. I became very jealous when other girls would message Cray and he was just as jealous about guys messaging me. We began saying very mean things to each other. Our relationship was based on sex and getting high. He was very much into "weed." His best friend, Dale, was very abusive towards his girlfriend and very controlling. I convinced my parents to allow Cray to live with me. My parents were never in agreement with my ideas, but they knew that if I did not get my way I would spiral downward even worse than I already was. My parents planned a cruise for our family and they allowed me to bring Cray along. I think, honestly, my parents were just happy that I had calmed down and stayed with one guy. While we were on the cruise, Cray and I began having an argument while my cousin, BeBe, and my little brother were with us. Suddenly, Cray slapped me very hard across the face. I was stunned. I could not believe what had just happened. Cray apologized and made up with me later. The rest of the cruise was fairly smooth.

The relationship went from bad to worse. Cray would punch me whenever we would have an argument and he started becoming more and more controlling. He would dictate what I would wear and became very jealous about any men who came around me, which was nearly all the time considering Cray always wanted to go smoke "weed" with his guy friends. Luckily they had girlfriends who I could chill with when he would smoke. The abuse became so bad I would walk with my head down, looking at my feet, because I could expect a punch to the face if a man crossed our way. Cray would say, "You were looking at that man again." It became a daily thing for me to have bruises all over my body and have to hide them. I loved the fact that Cray had long hair because when he would abuse me, I would grab it and try my best to fight him back.

The abuse continued for a year and Cray did not care if his friends saw him abuse me. For example, one time I was playing a joke on Cray. We were at the park with his friends and I had shaken a soda up so it would explode when he opened it. I thought it was harmless and I use to love playing jokes and having a good laugh. However, when he opened the soda and it exploded, Cray became enraged. I thought he was playing at first, so I started running playfully, but when I looked back and saw his face, I realized he was furious.

Cray grabbed me by my hair and jerked me to the ground kicking me three times saying, "Don't ever embarrass me like that again!"

One of his friend's whose name was Darrin ran up and said, "Are you serious, Man? She was just playing around."

I felt like I needed to stay with Cray to show people I could be dedicated and settle down.

One night Dale's girlfriend, Kate, asked me to go to the club with her. I was underage, being only fifteen years old. Dale convinced Cray that he should let me go with Kate so the two of them could do guy things. Reluctantly, Cray agreed to let me go. Kate dressed me up so that I looked about eighteen, which was the drinking age on the island. We arrived at the club and I began drinking a lot of different types of alcohol. In just a little over an hour I was already very intoxicated. Kate suggested that we should dance with some guys. So I started dancing with a guy named Ty. A couple of hours later, Kate and I went home to our boyfriends' houses. At the time Cray had moved to his sister's house. Now I was totally flesh-based with Cray, which means absolutely no God, just flesh, sex, drugs and no worries about life and consequences. The next morning I awoke to Cray answering a phone call. Evidently his sister's boyfriend, Iggy, had seen me dancing with Ty at the club. Cray looked very calm, considering the news he just heard. I knew how absolutely jealous he was. Cray walked over to his broken PS2 remote control with the wires hanging out of the cord. I was lying in Cray's bed naked. Suddenly that look Cray would always get before beating me up came to his face. That look told me, "I am going to teach you a lesson you will never forget." He stripped the plastic from the cord until it was all wire. He walked over and began whipping me with it. I had no way to fight back. I could only scream with every sting of the wires as they hit my back and face. While Cray whipped me I screamed out, "Jesus help me!" After about fifteen minutes Cray finished beating me. I could barely move. I had welts and blood all over my body. He told me to go in the shower. Cray then told me we needed to have sex to make up. I was so caught up in my flesh that the only thing I knew to do to numb all the emotions and all the pain was to have sex.

Some time after that I found out Cray was cheating on me and I lashed out at him. However, I never let myself get head over heels in love with Cray because I promised myself I would never let a man hurt me or have my heart again. So I sought revenge. I figured if I was getting beaten because Cray always assuming I was cheating on him then I might as well just do it. So I began sleeping with other men and let my flesh totally take over, even though deep down I knew I was damaging myself more and making myself feel even more worthless. I began drinking all the time and staying drunk. Cray and I eventually broke up after he did some soccer kicks to my ribs and broke some of my teeth. Personally, I did not even let it phase me. I knew I was not really in love with him. Even though deep down I still had that dream of wanting a great guy, but I forgot that God was suppose to be involved. I was still angry at God. I asked God, "Why Me?"

Honestly, I had really great friends. One was a totally relaxed "hippie" named Celest. She was just happy all the time. My other "Best Friend" was a coworker named Bri, who was just tough as hell, but nicer than ever to me. Eventually, I met an awesome girl from the States named Riz. She was one of the funniest girls you could ever meet. They always helped me. Even though my life style was not the best, they liked me for me.

After that horrible relationship with Cray I went back on my lust spree and started using all types of drugs. Just about anything to keep me numb to it all. I was in and out of short relationships, even dated girls!

One guy, named Joey, that I had cheated on Cray with had seen me at a bar one day. I was over intoxicated and waiting on my new boy toy to show up. Chase was not answering his phone though, which made me drink more. I hated feeling unwanted. Joey knew me from my lust state and was very aggressive. That's why I stopped having anything to do with him. He would get me so drunk and drugged. Half of the things that happened when I was with him I was too drugged to remember. Joey came up and tried to talk to me.

I said, "Listen, I am waiting for my new guy, Chase, ok?"

Joey replied, "Oh, I think I know him. Yea, he is at my house." I was very drunk and obviously very confused. Joey was with two guys. He ended up convincing me that Chase was at his house. So I went with Joey and his friends.

As we arrived at his house I began looking for Chase. To my surprise, Chase was nowere in sight, but ten very rough looking guys were. Suddenly Chase showed up. Chase just looked at me and walked off saying, "Stay with them!" I tried going after Chase, but I was too drunk! I did not know my way even out of the yard.

I ran up to Joey and asked, "What did you tell Chase?"
Joey replied, "Oh, nothing, just drink a beer."

I drank the beer and then asked, "Ok, so I drank the beer. Will you take me home or at least to somewhere I know?" Now most of the guys had already left, but Joey and his two friends were still there.

Joey picked up a large machete and said with a chuckle, "Oh, you are not going anywhere." I felt that uneasy feeling in the pit of my stomach. So I did what anyone would do, I tried to run, but they grabbed me and Joey held the machete to my back and said, "Get inside the house!"

I was trying my best not to be put in that house. It was one of those houses that you just knew some pretty wicked stuff had taken place. I grabbed the doorframe as they tried to jerk me inside. I kept kicking and trying not to lose my grip, but then they all grabbed me. They grabbed my legs and arms I lost my grip. I heard the front door closing and being locked. I screamed. They all looked so evil. They were laughing and having so much fun seeing me in total fear. I was in the middle of this so-called living room, which was just a room with a couch. In my mind I knew I needed to stay away from the bedrooms. They were all surrounding me like a pack of wild lions before they pounce on their prey. Suddenly I felt a sharp sting and major pain on my legs. Joey had slapped me with the machete. The minute that happened one of them rushed up and grabbed me from behind. Then another one grabbed my legs so I could not kick. I wondered how it was even fair that I was only five feet tall and 120 pounds and each of the guys were 150-170 pounds and close to six feet. I screamed and began to cry. They dragged me into the bedroom. Joey had my arms behind my back then his other friend held my legs and the other got on top. I couldn't believe it was happening. Joey and his other friend laughed while their friend raped me, like it was so amusing to them. It was so brutal I literally felt like animals were raping me.

After they each had their way with me, they let me go. As Joey opened the door he said, "See, it wasn't that bad."

I ran as fast as I could down the street trying to find the main road. It was one of those neighborhoods where if you took one wrong turn you would be wandering around for hours. After about five minutes of running as fast as I could I found the main road and headed straight to the police station.

Suddenly, they pulled up next to me in one of their cars and Joey asked, "Where ya going now?"

I lied and said, "I am going to get picked up and go home." I had no idea what horrible things would happen to me if they knew I was going to the police. I was a total wreck. I was missing a shoe, my clothes were disheveled and I was in pain. I was also as angry as ever because I could not do anything about what just happened. They just drove off and waited for a couple seconds to see where I was going. Of course I played it off and made it seem like I was just going to sit by the cemetery and wait for a ride. However, the minute I saw them drive off, I ran to the police station, walked in and reported that I was raped. The police took pictures, took my clothes, and well, you know the whole procedure. Except these were island cops, so their tactics were a little slow. They said they needed a rape kit and the exam would be done the next day, which I thought at the time was stupid. They do not have a special rape team nor officers on the island that show compassion when this kind of stuff happens, so you feel alone. On top of all that, two days later I found my beloved pit bull chopped open and dead. I am sure the guys must have found out I went to the cops.

I did not pursue bringing any charges against them because I felt afraid and all alone.

I began using the drug called "ecstasy" quite often. I used all kind of drugs like "uppers and downers," "weed" and of course consumed a lot of alcohol. I did not look to God for comfort. I liked staying numb because the memories hurt less.

About a month after that terrible rape, I met a guy named Taz at a bar that I was very well known at. It was the bar that Celest liked; however, Celest was no longer a hippie. She was now a full-blown, hardcore babe, as beautiful and feisty as ever.

I was now sixteen, and Taz was a lot older. I did not ask him how old he was at the time. (Later, I found out he was thirty-one.) Taz was decked out with gold jewelry and had lots of money. He was one of the biggest drug dealers in his district. I now wanted someone who would make sure that no one could ever hurt me again, and well, I thought he fit the description. I thought he was single the first night we went out drinking, only to find out he was actually still with his child's mother. It was a real shock. He had her move out and me move in. I was his new trophy. I should have known better, but I didn't. We went out every night and got high all the time. It was always his treat. Taz was so nice at first. Then, as always, his true colors began to show. He started getting drunk and roughing me up. He would flirt in front of me with other girls and leave me at home. He would go to the club saying he needed some time with the boys.

Chapter Two

"Love suffers long, and is kind; love does not behave itself unseemly, seeks not her own, is not easily provoked, and thinks no evil…"

I Corinthians 13:4,5

I remember one night crying in the shower saying, "God, please let him be the last guy. I do not want to keep jumping in and out of relationships. I am so tired."

After a while, whenever Taz and I would get drunk and I argued with him, he would choke me until I passed out. He would put me in headlocks until I lost consciousness. Taz soon insisted he wanted to have threesomes with my friends and I. I started becoming distant with him. I was so full of anger. It became a hurt game. Taz would dance with girls and I would show up and dance with guys. We'd fight then have make up sex. I started going out with my best friends while I was still living with Taz. His family loved me and were very nice people.

My Best friend, Bri, did not like Taz because of how he treated me. She would ask, "Girl, what are you doing with him." Well, honestly, the choking became punching whenever

I told Taz I was leaving him. I would just stay as high and drunk as I could. Deep down I knew I was unhappy, but when you keep yourself numb for so long you eventually do not care about your future.

Whenever I was clear headed enough I began thinking that I had a thing for guys that either did not have their fathers around or their fathers abused their mothers. I realized that I always wanted to somehow "fix them" and show them love. While I was with Taz, I started dating a girl again on the side. Just simple kisses. However, Taz found out and found it intriguing. Taz would try to get us to have a threesome and I always said no. Eventually I started to realize my spirit was dying and I was all flesh. I felt empty and worthless. Taz would sometimes tell me, "You're just a bitch I found on the street." I hated that I would always end up with that title no matter how much I tried in relationships. I would always be condemned about my past.

It was hard living with a full time drug dealer. You never knew when police would raid the yard, or who was lurking around or even what would happen if one of his drug deals went bad. I was so sick of the life I was living.

One day I became very ill. I could barely breathe, my throat was so swollen and I was extremely weak.

Taz left me in bed that day and said, "I will be back in a little bit."

After about two hours I felt even sicker. I called Taz and asked, "Hey, Babe, could you take me to the hospital? I am very sick."

He responded, "Call one of your friends. I am busy buying myself some shoes."

I hung up on him in mid conversation. I thought what a selfish prick he was. I called Bri and I asked her to come pick me up. She was there in about fifteen minutes. I told her to take me the bar where I knew Taz was. I always knew when Taz was drunk. So when Bri and I arrived there, of course Taz was there, drunk with one of his guy friends and another girl.

I walked up and said, "Give me my gold chain." I was so furious over how much he did not care about me being so sick. I went with Bri to her house where we smoked about two spliffs (marijuana cigarettes).

She asked, "You still want to go to the hospital awa?" In proper English that means, "Are we still going to the hospital?"

I said, "Na, man, I'm gonna thug this out." I always paid no mind when I got sick and I was angry. I said, "We going out tonight and I gonna get you and I wasted, ma."

Bri laughed and said, "Ok, Chargey." It was a little nickname because I was high or drunk all the time and on the island "charged" means you are either one of the two. So, we began getting ready and of course I wore the shortest dress I could.

Bri and I walked down her stairs and when we saw her mom she said "You guys look nice. Be careful now."

Bri laughed and said, "Ok, mommy."

We arrived at one of our favorite clubs. It was fifteen dollars for all you could drink and they never asked for my ID. I was only seventeen, but Bri was twenty-one. I had all types of different drinks. Soon I was totally drunk and out of nowhere Taz appeared, of course, he was drunk as well. I was ignoring him even though he began dancing with girls. I began getting more and more enraged. Downing drink after drink and building as much anger as I could. I was turning into a ticking time bomb.

It wasn't but a few minutes later when I saw Taz leaving with a girl. Oh, yes, my time bomb went boom! I ran down the stairs of the club yelling at Taz with every bad word in the book.

Bri came running behind me and said, "Let's go! He is a fool! Just leave him. He is just trying to get you embarrassed and mad."

Just then I unleashed all of my anger on her. I knew she had a rough relationship as well, so I bashed her with it. I said, "You do the same thing with your guy, so leave me alone! I am going to my man's house." She knew I was very drunk and very upset. This was the first time since we became friends that we argued. Then again, I guess you can say it was not even an argument. She did not say one mean thing to me.

She said, "Come on, I will cancel my plans and you can sleep at my house with me. I need to do something really serious tomorrow and I need you with me for this."

I continued shouting, "Listen, I am going to my man's house." I did not even think to ask her what the serious thing was. I was too drunk to even give it thought. I started walking down the road to Taz' house.

She chased me in her car saying, "Come on. Get in the car. You are too drunk." I didn't want to get in her car. I was focused on one thing and one thing only; to get to Taz! I started hitching for a ride when suddenly an old friend saw me and stopped. I jumped in his car and went to Taz' house. He did not show up until two hours later.

Bri called the next morning. I was still hung over.

She asked, "You good now?"

I laughed and said, "Yeah, Girl, I was drunk as ever! Please let me buy you lunch for being such an ass to you."

She laughed and said, "All right, but I've got to go do that thing first I was telling you about last night. I will call you when I get back."

I asked, "What is it? What do you have to do?"

She did not tell me then, she just replied, "When I get done, then I will tell you."

Well, lunchtime came. I tried calling her, but there was no answer. Evening came and still no answer. I thought the way I acted toward her the night before that maybe she was mad at me. Two days went by and still no reply to my calls or texts. I knew that wasn't like her. I began calling her other close friends. No one had heard from her. Then I found out that she never showed up for work. I told my mom that something was terribly wrong. We both worked for my mother, and Bri never missed a day of work. We went to the police to report her missing. They just said, "She's probably with some man." My mother and I were both angry at their reply. I told Taz and he said the same thing.

Rumors began to fly that she was shot and killed. I refused to believe it and told people they were crazy. My mother and I put up posters with her picture. Finally, on the sixth day, I heard the police had found the car that Bri was last seen driving. It was on a long, lonely stretch of road near the prison farm. They discovered it the night before. Her family was there looking for answers to what might have happened to her.

That night I prayed and said, "Jesus, I know I hardly talk to You, but if you could please show me what happened to Bri." That night I had the scariest dream of my life. I dreamed she was running from a guy with long dread locks in his hair. She was running in the woods, which is like a mini jungle. She was running scared and she fell. Then I saw the man with the dread locks had a machete in his hand. He lifted it up and swung it at her. I awoke in absolute fear and confusion.

I was due at work that day. Taz dropped me off. When I walked into work no one wanted to look at me. Everyone looked sad. I just walked past everyone to the back of the store. I glanced at my father and mother. Even they did not want to look me in the eyes.

Finally, my father spoke. "Honey, they found Bri."

I was overjoyed. I said, "Oh, thank God! Where is she?"

My dad replied sadly, "Honey, she is gone."

I was confused and asked, "Gone? Where is she? At the hospital or did she leave the island?"

He answered, "She is dead, Honey. I am so sorry."

I could not believe what he had just said. I yelled at him, "You're a liar! That's not true! It can't be true." Tears flooded my eyes and I felt like I couldn't breathe. I grabbed one of the flyers on the store door with the picture of Bri and ran outside. I sat on a bench looking at Bri's picture in total disbelief. I began calling all of her other friends.

I said, "Yo, this isn't true, right?"

However, one by one they each said, "Yeah, man, she's gone." Suddenly, the color of the world around me turned gray and I was in a world that had no color any more.

The gruesome details came out. It was her family that found her body. It was lying decomposed in the bush, on a dirt trail. No, it was not the police who found her. Her family found her.

I called Taz and told him. I said, "I need your support right now, Taz. I feel like I am losing my mind." He said, "I think you need to be alone."

I became angry and bitter. My mind began racing on what happened and why. The first week after I received the news I totally shut down. I continued calling Bri's phone. I still looked for her. I did not want to accept that she was gone. I hated the fact that the last time I saw her I was yelling at her. If only I had gone with her to do that serious thing, then maybe this would not have happened to her. I blamed myself. Maybe, just maybe, if I had been with her I could have prevented her death.

I was back at my parent's house during this time. My parents lived about ten minutes from where her body was found. The minute I heard the police pulled the yellow tape down on the murder site I went there. I wanted to know what happened. I was determined to figure it out. As I walked down the trail I had never been before, I saw things I had seen in my dream. There were the two big rocks that she had run by in the dream, and the same view of those leaves. I approached where Bri's body had been found. I just saw the outline of where her body was and my precious friend's dried blood. I fell to the ground and laid myself on her dried blood.

I was crying and screamed out, "God, give her back. Take me instead, please!" Then I sobbed, "Why her? What did she do to die like this? How could you let this happen?" I lay there for a while and then walked over to the shed were she was attacked. I saw her bloody handprints and sat there trying to imagine what she must have gone through while she was in there. The images of my precious friend trying to run from her killer or maybe even killers caused me to go into a complete mental breakdown.

Two nights before her funeral, an ex-boyfriend of hers and his new girlfriend tried to run my mother and I off the road. I realized they must have had something to do with it.

On the day of Bri's funeral, I went with Liza, one of Bri's close friends, and some of my close friends. I kept staring at

Bri's coffin and thinking that could not really be her in there. I could not accept it was real. I became severely depressed, had severe anxiety and worst of all, I hated God!

My mother told me the day of Bri's funeral that I had to leave the island. At first I thought maybe she just thought it would be best for me. However, the truth is it was because I was the last one seen with Bri the night before she was killed. My home was in the district where she was killed and the police said they received word that someone had hired a couple of "hit men" to kill me. So they all thought it was best that I got off the island. I only wish that I had known more information. I wish I knew what the killers thought I knew. If I did, then I would not be losing my mind trying to solve Bri's murder, which had so little clues and left every one wondering who did it and why. I wanted answers. I did not care if they wanted me dead, I just wanted to know who did it, what happened and why. Nevertheless, I did as my mother suggested and Taz came with me. My mother told him not to leave me alone because of how mentally unstable I was. I was given antidepressants and was smoking an ounce of weed a day. I had to stay numb to the point that my life was without color.

Taz and I arrived in Florida and stayed at a motel. Taz considered it an awesome vacation. I just kept drinking and staying numb. My mind never rested. I was constantly trying to figure out who killed my best friend and why. That's all I thought about. Taz got me a fake ID so I could go into the clubs with him, which only worked twice before I almost got arrested. I began asking Taz what he knew and if he heard anything.

He said, "I heard it was maybe a guy from the prison."

Then over the next couple of weeks people on the island evidently started talking about one of her ex-boyfriends. He and his new girlfriend were the same ones who tried to run me off the road with my mom before I left. I kept trying to piece the puzzle together. I hated being in that hotel room and not being able do anything about Bri's murder. I wanted revenge! I wanted to kill the people who took her life; the people who took the color from my world and stole my happiness.

One night Taz said, "I'm going across the road for a little while to have a drink." Well, I knew what that meant. It meant I was going to be in the room alone because my ID had been taken away from me.

I said, "All right. You're coming back soon though, right? You know what I'm going through, so please don't be long."

He left. An hour went by and then two hours. After four hours, my mind began racing around with horrible thoughts about my best friend. I was literally losing my mind. Sitting on the bed, I felt so alone. I wanted the pain of missing Bri to stop. My mind was filled with the thoughts of what I would have done if I had been there and the guilt of never being able to tell her how sorry I was for the first argument we ever had. Our first, and last.

I glanced across the room and noticed a steak knife on the sink. I thought to myself that Bri was gone and it was too much pain for me to bear. I began to think *this is the end*. I said, "I am with a man who doesn't even care what I am going through and that I am alone." I walked over and grabbed the knife. I looked at my wrist and suddenly began cutting them deeper and deeper. It felt so perfectly right. It felt like the pain was flowing out of me. I was numb to everything, even this sharp knife slitting my wrist. Suddenly the thought went through my mind to sing *Jesus Loves Me*. I thought, *How could that help me and why do I need to sing that song?* I even thought how totally inappropriate it was to sing *Jesus Loves Me* while trying to kill myself. Nevertheless, I started singing it. The moment I started singing I dropped the knife. I knew it was God saying, "No, my Child, this is not how you die."

Suddenly, an uneasy feeling came over me and I felt as if Taz knew something about Bri's murder that he was not telling me. I felt that I was with "the enemy."

I called my mother and said, "Mom, I need to come home."

To my surprise she said, "Ok." As soon as I got off the phone with her I heard Taz outside the room. It was 5:00 in the morning. I opened the door to see him staggering up the stairs.

He said, "Oh, Baby, I had such a good time." I was instantly furious with him. I threw everything in the room to the ground and screamed, "I hate you and what you have put me through." I waited until he fell down onto the bed and grabbed that same knife and put it to his back. Pressing it up against him I said, "I should kill you!"

His eyes got big and he yelled, "What are you doing? Are you crazy?"

I laughed and answered, "You have no idea how crazy I have become." Taz then turned around and punched me twice in the head. I did not care though. I thought *I will find out what happened to Bri if it is the last thing I do.*

The next morning I told Taz I was leaving and going back to the island. He did not ask if we were still going to be together. He just knew we weren't going to be a couple anymore, even though we did not address the issue. My parents had arranged that I would meet up with my sister Marie in a different part of Florida and spend a couple of days with her before going back to the island. So I got on the plane in Orlando and flew to Fort Lauderdale.

Let me help you understand the mental state I was in at the time. I was not scared of anything anymore, or anybody. I felt like I had nothing to lose.

When I got on the plane to Fort Lauderdale, I sat next to this guy. We began having a really nice conversation. He seemed really nice. He invited me to go smoke some weed with him when we arrived in Fort Lauderdale. To a sensible girl, who was not in the middle of a complete mental breakdown, that would have been a ridiculously bad idea. However, I really did not care. I just wanted to stay numb and get high now because I knew that for the next two days I was going to have no weed.

We landed in Fort Lauderdale. The guy asked me, "So, are you going to come with me and chill?"

I replied, "Yeah, I just need you to drop me off at my hotel afterwards. I have to meet my sister there."

So, I got into his car and we started driving. I did not honestly even think about what could possibly happen. I mean considering the fact I just met this guy on the airplane and no one knew when I landed that I was even with this guy, it was a potentially serious situation. We arrived at his apartment and it was a little rough, but I thought, *why not?* He pulled out some very beautiful weed and began rolling a very big blunt.

He asked, "So are you ready to go on a drive and light this?" I nodded my head and smiled. We started driving and smoking the blunt. The weed he had was very strong. I was amazed because after taking only four puffs, I was completely stoned. To me that was a mission accomplished. I mean that

I got to be numb again, just like the way I felt about life. So I was satisfied.

Now I was supposed to arrive at the hotel to meet my sister fifteen minutes after I landed because the hotel was not far from the airport. However, by the time I was dropped off, three hours had passed. I remember walking into the hotel while I was on "cloud nine."

I asked the receptionist while laughing, "Would you happen to know what room my sister would be in?" From the look that the receptionist gave me I think she knew I was pretty stoned. In the midst of our conversation, I heard loudly clicking heels coming up quickly behind me. When I turned around I saw my big sister with a panicked look on her face. I said, "Hey sis!"

She asked sternly, "Where the hell have you been?"

I chuckled and answered, "I'm here right." Now my big sister was also a very short person, 5'1" to be exact, so there was always humor in my sister being a concerned big sister when she was only an inch taller than me.

She looked into my eyes and asked, "Are you high?"

I responded, "Of course."

We spent two days together just shopping and eating at restaurants. My family always knew how to help me try to forget that my life was falling apart, just by keeping me busy and trying their best to always be available. I thanked my sister for the two days and off I went back to the island; back to the unbearable reality that I wish I could escape.

The day I returned, I was greeted by Celest. We got wasted that night at a festival called batabano, which is a huge event that is about drinking, dancing and food. The whole time I was out, though, I kept thinking about Bri and how much everything about the island reminded me of her. I hated it, and of course whenever I was around Celest and Riz I always feared of losing them as well.

After that night, I went into a state of thinking that I just did not want to enjoy life anymore. So I just sat in my room all day popping antidepressants, Xanax and smoking weed. I sat on my bed, listening to music while staring out at the ocean, trying to find a reason why life was even worth living anymore. Whenever I did leave my room it was just to get weed and cigarettes. I did not bother to talk to God anymore. I had reserved myself to the belief that I was going to have to be forever high and numb.

Some days, I would have my other friends come see me and smoke weed, cigarettes, and just listen to music to chill out. Other days I would just cry all day. The loss of never being able to see one of my best friends again hurt me so bad emotionally that I actually felt physical pain. It felt like I had open-heart surgery while wide-awake, and the knife was still in me. I had become numb to life itself, always asking God, *Why her?*

I had an old fling come over and I just wanted sex from him. I did not even leave my room to go to his house. When an urge came to have sex, I would just call someone I had no relationship with and for whom I had no emotions. I had no love to give. I was fully numb to it all.

Then one night I had a dream about Bri. She was sitting on one of the stones on the trail where she was killed. As I approached her she looked up at me and said, "I am ok and I miss you." Then she hugged me. I awoke from the dream still smelling her perfume.

I cried all that morning, missing her so much and dialing her number over and over again just to hear her voice on her voicemail. One of my cousins and her girlfriend began staying in my room with me. My cousin, Rose, and her girlfriend, Thais, stayed with me and were there 24/7. Everyone was becoming very worried about my mental state. I hardly left my room and if I had weed and cigarettes I would stay in there for a month.

My mother told me to read a book called *The Shack*. I picked it up and started reading. I soon began understanding God and my life more. Then one day God gave me a brief memory of Bri. I had forgotten all about this. It was a week before she was killed. Bri, one of her close friends and I were all having lunch. Bri's friends were different. We all never really hung out together before. But that day we did. We were all eating lunch when Bri said something very strange. She said she wanted to slow down the partying and felt like getting back to God. We all laughed at the time and said, "Oh sure!" However, during this memory flashback, God spoke to me and said she was indeed ready to give her heart back to Him. Of course, I still asked God why this happened to her, but some things we will never understand I guess.

I did become very afraid though to get into relationships with men. Bri's murder trial was about to begin. Three people were involved. One was a prisoner who was her ex-boyfriend's uncle. The one who was the nephew and his girlfriend were the same two who tried to chase me off the road.

One night my cousin, Rose, and Thais told me I needed to get out of the house.

I said, "Alright. I know I am going to hate it though."

Rose replied, "Get dressed. We are getting you out."

We arrived at a bar that was connected to a nightclub. Of course, I was high and drugged out on Xanax. I began drinking as well. I still needed to be numb and live in my flesh. Everything was still too raw and real. I was making out with girls in the club. I thought a girl would not be as dangerous as a guy. I would not have to be afraid of a girl. But I continued drinking and my flesh took over completely. I began dancing. Suddenly, Ty appeared behind me and started dancing with me. He started whispering sweet things in my ear. He said, "I have really liked you for a very long time. You are the girl of my dreams." I giggled thinking how honored I was that a guy would say that. I was completely in the flesh drunk, high and missing Bri so much.

Ty asked, "Will you come home with me?" I thought I felt so alone and numb that I could not hurt any worse than I did because there was no worse hurt than what I was feeling.

I answered, "Hell yea." I knew deep down I was not into living at all. I remember leaving the club with Ty and while I was in the back seat of the car Ty's friend was driving I prayed to God quietly and said, "God, protect the people in the world from all this evil."

Ty and I smoked some weed once we got to his house, we had sex, and I remember how pointless it all felt. I just wanted to feel some kind of emotion other than my grief. Ty told he loved me. I just looked at him and smiled. On the inside I thought *Love? What is love?* I related it to the love I had for Bri and that no one could ever have that part of my heart, and no one could ever fix it. Honestly, I felt afraid of men and what they could do to women.

The next morning I awoke early and left, not caring much about what had happened. I just wanted to get home. I mean most of my days I would try to piece together Bri's murder. That was all that mattered, but Ty wanted a relationship and did not want to leave me alone. He called all the time and would show up at my house. I told him I wasn't ready, but he insisted that he knew the state I was in and loved me regardless. I knew it was a bad idea, but I thought if he knows that I am just going to stay broken and numb, and he still wants to be with me, well, then why not.

I would work from 10 a.m. to 10 p.m. because I wanted stay busy. My parents had two stores at different centers. I had not stepped foot into the one I used to work at with Bri since she was killed. I worked at the Westshore one, which was on the west part of the island. Ty would always want to hang out and stay at my place while I was at work. I had gotten my own apartment, but I really did not want to be in a relationship. A couple of months went by and Ty became possessive.

Chapter Three

"Just because you can't find someone who treats you right, doesn't mean you should be someone who doesn't."

-Unknown

He would put on this front around his friends that he was in control of me. That caused me to break up with him all the time. I did not like that he would act so differently when his friends were around. I was going through too much to be treated like this.

When his friends were over one day Ty thought it would be funny to burn me with a cigarette.

I yelled, "Why the hell are you doing that kind of shit?"

He snickered to himself and said, "Oh, baby it was just an accident."

I noticed he started trying to show he had control over me in front of his friends, which I could not stand because he was totally different when they were not around. He was always asking me for money and weed. I felt like I was nothing more to him than his possession.

I had this younger friend named Riley whom I had met at my store. She had just moved down from Florida. Every time she wanted me to come over Ty wanted to go so I never had time to be alone with my new friend.

Whenever Celest would come see me I made Ty stay inside so I could talk with her in peace. He would always try to belittle me around my friends and I just got to the point that I had no more tolerance for it. Every time I would break up with him he would end up coming to my house at night, wait till I got home and beg me to take him back.

Ty would say, "Baby, I am so sorry. I keep forgetting about the state you are in and your condition."

You see, after Bri died I was diagnosed with posttraumatic stress disorder. I was depressed and chemically imbalanced. I really did not care when Ty and I would break up because I was numb. Life did not change one bit with or without him.

I remember one time Ty was on his way to my house and apparently he had "butt dialed" my phone. I heard him talking to his friend Mika saying, "She's got a lot of money you know. I'm going to have money all the time."

Mika asked, "So does she give you money?"

Ty laughed, "Almost whenever I want it."

I just sat there, listened for a while and hung up. I started thinking how Ty use to always ask me for money saying he needed money for fines that were due in court. I was numb, not in love with him, but I was and always have been kind and considerate. I never told Ty I heard the conversation. But I knew that he was now not only with me for my looks, but also my money. Which at the time I really did not care. I was not in love, I was in the flesh! He would usually treat me nice except when he got around his friends. I started getting very distant from him. I use to go to work, call Celest or Riz and go get drunk with them. I had total control over Ty and my relationship. I guess because I was the one who did not care about it. I know it sounds heartless, but I had no love to give and I had warned him before we got together. I told him I was numb and had no feelings. You can't love when you are already hurt by life and live in the flesh. Nothing makes you better.

Around the seventh month mark of Ty and my relationship, I broke up with him and dated this guy named Dale for two days. Dale would often say he wanted to be in a relationship and would come around now and then. He was still with Kate on the "down low." We only lasted for two days, however, and he went back with Kate. Ty of course wanted to get back together.

During this period that I was with Ty I was going through Bri's murder trial. It was so hard listening to all of the details of how she had died. I remember sitting in court holding her mother's hand and having to listen to the details of the autopsy. My best friend, Bri, was chopped fifteen times and bled to death for nearly a day. Bri's family and I became very close during this period of time. Liza and I had also become close as well. She was one of Bri's other close friends.

About a week before the one-year anniversary of Bri's death, I was talking to Celest on the phone. She was back in Florida. I was going to leave Ty and go to live with her in Florida. Celest said, "Do not go and get pregnant."

I just laughed and replied, "Me? Never." Celest would be on the island for a short period of time and then she would return to Florida for a while. She always came and went. We pretty much always had a long distance friendship. I remember around the five-month mark of Ty and I dating I was home with my parents and I went out into the front yard of my house just as high as ever. Suddenly I saw a car stop. Celest jumped out and came running towards me. She jumped on me and hugged me. She always knew how to make a smile pop on my face. I knew I was going to go and live with her.

On the day of the one-year anniversary of Bri's death, I went to the pharmacy with Riley and took a pregnancy test. Boom! I was pregnant. I am not going to lie, I was actually happy about it. I felt like maybe God was giving me new life in place of Bri being gone. But honestly, I was not sure how Ty would react. I mean I did not have any feelings for him and had not given him my heart at all. I was not trying to have a baby, but I guess that's how unexpected life is.

I told Ty I was pregnant and surprisingly he was happy. I said, "Listen, I know I have not been a great girlfriend, so if you are going to use this time of me being pregnant as pay back for anything I have done tell me now. I rather have us just not do this and me not be pregnant if you are going to treat me badly."

Ty responded, "Babe, I would never do that. I love you and I know how much you have been through with Bri being gone. I am going to take great care of you and our baby."

Now I was only 18 at the time and I thought *well, all right, I guess I will settle with Ty and try to love him*. But, before I could even begin to love Ty, he began to change. I was very sick during my first month of pregnancy and Ty started acting very shady. He began partying a lot and always making up lies of where he was. One time he said, "Baby, I am going to the grocery store with my mom. I will call you when we get done and you can come pick me up." Well, something in me knew he was lying. So I called my little brother, Seth, and my friend Riley and asked them to come with me where Ty lived. Ty was living in a very rough part of the island. I showed up there and I felt like I should go into the bar. I went around the back of the bar where rooms where. These rooms were used for the bar girls to hook up with guys.

Not to my surprise, there was Ty with a girl. He looked like a deer in the headlights. I caught them with clothes on but from the expressions on their faces I just knew. Ty then yelled, "What the hell you doing here? You are dumb."

I yelled back, "I'm dumb? No, you are just mad that you got caught."

Ty got up in my face and started saying some very mean things. "You're such a stupid bitch! You are lucky you're pregnant, Whore!"

My Brother, Seth, heard Ty say this and all of a sudden my brother popped around the corner and yelled, "You ever talk to my sister like that again, you pussy, we are going to have some serious issues."

Ty just looked at my brother. I said, "Come on, Riley and Seth, let's go."

We left in my car and drove back to my parents' house. I had started staying with my parents again once I found out I was pregnant. Ty sent me a text on my phone saying that he was sorry and that he loved me. I felt vulnerable being pregnant and being so sick. I accepted Ty's apology, but Ty continued with this behavior and coming to my parents' house drunk every night saying, "Oh, baby, I am not drunk. I love you." Ty tried to convince me to live at his house with his family once the baby arrived. I always told him no. Any time I would spend the night at Ty's house he would always be gone the next morning and would take my car. Ty started telling me all the time that he had more court fines, so I would give him $200 like it was nothing. I did not want the father of my child to be in jail. Now at that time I started hanging out with Liza. She was pregnant also. I told her that I knew my baby was going to be a girl.

Being pregnant made me try to fall in love with Ty, but he kept doing so many shady things. For example, some days I could not reach him all day long. Finally, he would call some time late at night. He would always make up some excuse and say something like, "Baby, my phone was not working all day."

He also started becoming very verbally abusive and every time I would say, "Fine, we are done." He would always come back begging me to be with him. When I was around three months pregnant it was one of those days that Ty was ignoring my calls. So I showed up at his house that night saw his mother and aunt outside.

I asked, "Where is Ty?"

His mother said, "He is inside lying down."

"Can you tell him I am outside?" All of a sudden Ty came out of the house and walked over to my car. Being pregnant, I was very emotional and angry. I asked him, "So where have you been all day that you can't answer your pregnant girlfriend's calls?"

He replied sarcastically, "Oh, you know, here and there. Everywhere really." I could smell the alcohol coming off his breath. A ton of thoughts began running through my head. I kept thinking *I am not even in love with him yet and I have been trying to fall in love.* I could not believe I was so sick and pregnant with his baby. He had begun being so demeaning to me, especially when he was in his neighborhood.

So I broke my train of thought and said, "I knew you were going to do this."

He laughed, "What are you talking about?"

"Don't worry, Ty, this will be the last time you disappoint me and take advantage of the fact that I am pregnant. I truly do not need you and I will raise this baby by myself." I saw Ty begin looking around to see if any of his guy friends were watching. Of course they were and they were all inquisitive.

So Ty put his finger in my face, "Who do you think you are talking to like that, Bitch?"

I yelled, "Stop trying to impress your little friends, Ty." He punched me in my face out of nowhere.

I jumped out of the car with my pregnant belly and all. I was furious, and was not going to stand for this kind of shit anymore. "Ok, Ty, I get it. You want to try me now that I am pregnant and can't fight you back. Tell you what, you are never going to see me or this child again."

Then Ty slapped me the hardest he could in my face. I tasted blood and it trickled down from my lip. Ty looked at me like he was shocked.

"Ok, Ty," I said. "You made your bed, now I hope you can sleep in it." I held my belly, got back in my car and sped off back to my parents' house. While I was driving home my anger began to build. I actually wanted to kill Ty.

I was about five minutes from my parents house when he texted me saying, "Baby, I am so sorry. I do not know what I just did. Are you ok?"

I texted back, "Do not worry about me." About two hours later I decided to call Ty and try to talk. Ty did not answer. I tried calling him about fifteen times with still no answer. I sat on my parents' couch crying with a busted lip. I told myself before I fell asleep from crying so much that this was the first and last time I will ever cry over Ty. The next morning I awoke bitter as ever. Ty had texted me twenty times saying he loved me so much. I turned off my phone, got dressed and went to Liza's house. Now Liza was a couple of months ahead of me in her pregnancy. She was smoking weed and cigarettes because she was stressed out with her son's father. She had a huge spliff rolled up. I was so upset and numb that I said, "Give me some." After taking three hits off the spliff my situation became easy to deal with. Weed was going to be my escape again, from life and from my pain.

Ty began showing up at my parents' house whenever they were out, trying to beg me back. I would always tell him no. He would always respond with a punch to the face while yelling nonstop.

I eventually got to the point where I would leave my parents' house every morning at 7:00 a.m and head to my cousin's or Celest's house. I would stay away all day until 12:00 a.m. smoking weed and eating. I also had a cousin named Jamie who was pregnant also. I looked to all of my friend's and family members for comfort, avoided seeing Ty day and night, hoping he would not show up at my parents' house when I would get home late. He would always bring me gifts and try to spend the night, but by the time we would lay down he would start abusing me. It was pointless to stay with him. I hated him. I began making sure I was never home so I never had to deal with him. I was working through my pregnancy and after work I would go smoke and stay with either one of my close girlfriends. Liza and I began getting close, eating lunch together all of the time. Deep down I knew Liza and I saw Bri in each other.

I remember a poem I wrote for Bri the year after her being killed I wrote it on her birthday and just how I was feeling about her being gone.

I awoke this morning trying to face another day
I look outside no color still just grey
Still in disbelief and great dismay
I wonder why my friend is not here till this day
A year later and my soul is still empty as can be
I begged God to send her back and let it be me
Who knew such a beautiful person would have to suffer this kind of death?
What I would have done to be there when she took her last breath
To say good-bye but I guess I was too late
So heavy on my heart to know she had to suffer this type of fate
What if she had come back when she said she'd be back in a while?
What if I still got to hear her jokes and see her smile?
Who knew such a beautiful person would have to suffer a death so vile?
The laughs, the memories, all the things we use to share
No one can explain yet why life is so unfair
Then she replied back to me she said I may be gone but I am still near
Live life like I did and never have fear
It may seem, but I'm not that far away so light my candles and please don't cry
For I am having my first birthday in the sky

Every time I shared this poem with someone they were always crying by the end. I did not mean to make them cry, but that was the only way I knew how to express how I was feeling and missing Bri. I actually enjoyed being high all of the time. Many people thought it was interesting that a pregnant woman chose to be alone. But when the person you are pregnant by is abusive and you have no feelings for them then it is easier doing it by yourself.

One day my mother spoke to me and said, "Honey, I want you to start reading scripture over your daughter in your belly." I was very bitter, not resting like a pregnant woman should towards the end of my pregnancy and I was avoiding Ty like the plague. I felt weird, like maybe I was supposed to look towards God. So I did. I began reading scripture and praying that my daughter would come out all right, despite me always smoking weed. I did not want to be with Ty, not only because he was abusing me while I was pregnant, but for my daughter's sake. I did not want her being raised around someone like that.

I could not get over the fact that he never considered that his daughter was in the body he was beating. I felt like if he did not want to respect her while she was in me then do not be around when she is out of me. Liza use to always think I was a little cold hearted for leaving him, but Liza was staying with her child's father who was the same. Celest, Riz, Jamie, Rose and Thais all agreed with my decision. They all saw the bruises Ty would leave on my body. Now Ty would also trick me sometimes to come see him. He would say that he had something for me I would show up in his neighborhood and the abuse would start. I remember when I was eight months pregnant with my daughter I went to Celest's house because she had a couple of guys and Riz over. I was eating and smoking weed with all of them. I felt comforted by them because all of our guy friends kept rubbing my belly. Even though I knew I was alone and felt numb I still found comfort being with my friends.

Not long after I started reading scriptures to my daughter, I began having dreams a couple of nights in a row that I knew that they were visions from God. I saw myself in one dream standing on the beach in front of my parents' house. I was looking out at the ocean and something in me felt a peace about Bri's death. I was wearing a white throwback t-shirt. Then I had another dream where I saw myself going on to a stage in California. It was a church I saw my daughter sitting next to my father. She was older, like maybe four or five years old. She had beautiful curly hair. A couple of weeks passed and one morning I awoke, read my bible like I always did each morning for the past month and yes, I still smoked weed. I walked out onto my parents' beach and I looked out at the ocean. I suddenly felt a peace that I hadn't felt since Bri was killed. I smiled, looked down and noticed I was wearing that white throwback t-shirt I was wearing in the first dream.

Life was starting to make sense again. I was reading my bible everyday, not feeling so alone and numb. I was actually having feelings for life again. I prayed God would bring the right man into my life to help me raise my daughter and I prayed that I would wait patiently until He did. I had found out from my doctor that week that I was going to need a C-section. I was a little scared at first, but I just kept praying.

Four days before I was going to go to the hospital to have my daughter, I heard a knock on my glass door. Now because I knew my daughter was to arrive soon I went into nesting mode. I wanted everything ready, which meant I would have to stay home. I walked to the glass door and opened my curtains. It was Ty. My whole body shook in fear.

Ty said, "Baby, open the door." Now I was home by myself and my parents were at work. I knew it was a bad idea if I let him in, but I knew if I didn't he would sneak in through a window and then that would be a guaranteed fight.

So I slowly opened the door. "Ty, what are you doing here?"

He answered, "I am your daughter's father. What do you mean? You have been avoiding me for months." Ty then stepped inside my room.

I said, "Ty, you need to go," and I began pushing him out of my room.

He then shoved me off and said, "I am not going anywhere. Stop telling me what to do." He began getting closer and closer to me. He tried to touch my stomach.

"Do not touch my stomach, Ty." He suddenly grabbed me by my throat and pinned me up against the wall. I could not breathe. I kept trying to ease his grip. I felt my daughter squirming in my stomach. I knew that my daughter and my air supply was cut off.

I began to pass out. Then, boom! My mother came flying through my bedroom door. "Let go of my daughter, Ty!" she screamed. Ty released me. I was trying to catch my breath as my mother began yelling at Ty. "Get out of this house!" She pushed Ty out of my room through the door he entered in, which took the argument outside onto our beach. I was still breathless, but I was concerned for my mom as I heard the argument escalating. I walked out my sliding glass door to see Ty getting very close to my mother and looking like he wanted to hit her.

I jumped in the middle, belly and all. "Do not ever approach my mother like that you mad awa!" (Which means, Are you crazy?) I shoved Ty as hard as I could away from my mother. "Leave, Ty, and do not ever come back." Ty's eyes began to fill up with tears. I did not care one bit. I refused to allow this any more in my life. Ty eventually left. My mother and I went back inside.

She asked, "Honey, are you ok? Do you need to go to the hospital?" I told her no. I felt my daughter kicking stronger than ever. It was like my daughter was saying I am proud of you mommy.

I wrote a journal for my daughter telling her about the abuse I went through with her father, explaining why I had to leave and why she was never going to know him. I went into the hospital three days later. I watched Christian television that night when I was in my hospital room. I was getting so excited about meeting my daughter. The next morning I awoke and was ready to meet her. They took me into surgery. My mom was there during the whole thing. She sprayed me with water mist and kept telling me comforting words. Then I saw the love of my life: my beautiful, brown-eyed daughter. I felt overjoyed. Most of all, God kept His promise to me. She was perfectly fine in health and beautiful. They rolled me back into my hospital room. I held my daughter for the first time. It was so precious. I called all my friends and let them know she was born. About fifteen minutes afterwards, an uneasy feeling came over me. Then I saw Liza walk through the door and right behind her was Ty. He had roses and chocolates with him. He was smiling, but I was not. I was furious!

I just looked at Liza wondering why she would bring him with her into the same room with my precious daughter, the life he had totally disregarded when she was in me. My mother walked in nearly at the same time.

She said, "No, Ty, you need to leave now."

"Mom, let me deal with this and step out for just a second." I was sharing a room with a sweet girl named Kisha and her friend Chia. They were still in the room. I looked at Ty.

He said, "Oh, she is so beautiful." I laughed and replied, "Yeah, she is. However, it is too bad that you did not think about that when you were abusing me, huh?" I was so bitter. The more I looked at my daughter and how beautiful she was the more I kept thinking that Ty did not care about her well being when I was pregnant. Then Ty walked over to her. I was bedridden and my body was still numb from the waist down. I put my arm out in front of him and said, "Do not touch my daughter."

"Are you serious?" Ty asked.

"Do you think you can waltz in here with roses and chocolates and think everything is fine?" I responded. "Get out now."

Ty frowned and began walking through the door and was gone. Liza said, "Oh, honey, he saw me and asked if you were in the hospital and I could not lie. He asked me to take him to get you all that stuff."

I said, "Yeah, well I do not want anything to do with him."

Deep down I was pissed that Liza would do that. I mean if she were really concerned and cared about me, why would she bring my abuser to the hospital? Liza left after that. Chia and Kisha said, "That was cold."

"If only you knew what he put me through, you would not think so." I gave the chocolates to Kisha and said, "Here. You have them. I truly did not want anything from him." I was bitter, and my anger started to boil over for him.

I left the hospital two days later with my new beautiful daughter, Lilly. The day I got home I got a call from Celest. She said, "Are you home?"

"Yes."

Within about five minutes I heard a knock at my front door and there was Celest. She always wore the cutest things. She was wearing a pair of blue and white furry slippers.

I laughed when I saw them. "Did you kill a smurf with bleach?"

"Of course I did!" We had a funny humor about our friendship, always popping corny jokes.

Chapter Four

"The Lord also will be a refuge for the oppressed, a refuge in times of trouble. And they that know thy name will put their trust in thee: for thou, Lord, hast not forsaken them that seek thee."

–Psalms 9:9, 10

For the first week of my daughter being home I was still reading my bible, but I felt kind of lonely and I was still smoking weed all of the time. Liza and I still talked and she was still with her son's father. I tried to put what she did behind me and never confronted her about it. I would go hang out at her house some days with my daughter.

About two weeks after giving birth to my daughter I was chilling at my house with my baby girl when I heard a knock on my glass door. It was Ty again. I was angry. I had forgotten to lock my glass door considering I was always high. Ty slid the door open and walked right into my house. My stitches were still in my stomach from my C-section so lucky for me I had enough weed to stay numb as ever physically, mentally and emotionally.

Ty walked over to our daughter.

"Don't you dare!" I screamed. Ty then squared off with me like he was going to hit me. I saw my sliding glass door behind him was still opened.

I let the anger of every time he hit me take over. I kicked him as hard as I could straight into his stomach. His body flew out of the opening of my glass door and down the two steps landing him on the beach. I slammed my glass door and locked it. I am not going to lie. I was totally shocked at how strong my kick was, and that my stitches had not ripped open. Now I knew I was supposed to be patient and let God bring the right guy for me to raise my daughter, but I let my flesh take over again. So now I was bitter and angry as hell. I wanted Ty to hurt as much as I did. I let my flesh take me into wanting revenge.

Two nights later, I went out to the club with Liza and I got drunk as ever. Of course, I saw Ty that night. He walked right past like he did not even know me. I was fine with that. I thought *Good! It helps me be more bitter and angry.*

The next morning Ty called me. "Baby, how are you?"

I responded, "Go away, Ty, you lousy piece of dust." Evidently Ty was drunk that night and did not notice me. A guy had smashed Ty's face with a brick and beat him up too. Since I was totally the in flesh, and bitter as ever, that knowledge of his beating put a smile on my face. I was letting anger and bitterness drive me. I began going out with Celest, as well. I wanted to find a man to help father my daughter. But now I had a new insecurity. I was scared about how men would look at me now that I had a daughter. I questioned whether or not I could find someone that would love me with a kid and would love her as well. I did not want to wait for God, He was taking way too long. I wanted a man to love my daughter and me. About three weeks after having my daughter, Celest invited me over to her house one night. Celest was right up the street from my house. So I asked my parents to watch my daughter and I went.

I knocked on Celest's front door. "Come in." I opened the door to find two guys sitting at Celest's table rolling up some weed. One of them was Celest's new boyfriend named Sy. He seemed very nice. The other one was his cousin. I introduced myself to him. He was shy, but cute. A smile that sparkled and arms buffer than ever, yeah, he was gorgeous. We had a little spark between us. We began talking over that week. His name was Jalus. Well, as soon as he told me his name, I remembered Liza telling me about a guy she was screwing while she was still with her son's father. She had mentioned that he was just a screw toy and his name was Jalus.

"Do you know Liza?"

He looked at me laughing and replied, "Yeah. Why?"

I pushed his arm off me. "I am sorry, but she is one of my close friends so I can't talk to you."

He replied, "She is with her son's father and ditched me. Why can't we talk?"

"Well, I am going to have to speak to Liza first. I like you, but I do not want to hurt my friend."

Celest agreed with me that it was a wise thing to do before pursuing anything with Jalus.

So the next day I called Liza. "Liza, can I come see you? I want to ask you something in person." I have always been the type of friend, who when needing to ask my friends something serious, wants to be face to face. So I drove to the other end of the island to meet with Liza. I picked her up a pack of cigarettes also. I loved treating my friends to anything they needed. I called Liza to let her know I was on my way and she said she was at a friend's house and for me to meet her there. I arrived, handed her the cigarettes and began smoking.

I said, "Liza, I have to ask you something."

"Ok, what is it?" she asked.

"Liza, I met this guy and he really likes me, but I found out that it is Jalus. But, listen, if you really like him and he means something to you then I will not talk to him anymore, ok?"

She laughed and replied, "Girl, I am still with my son's father. You go ahead."

"Are you sure? I do not want to get involved with Jalus if you have feelings for him."

"No, you are single and he is single, so go ahead, girl." I left that day happier than ever knowing that my friend was ok with it. Now the island is very small so you are lucky if you do not end up dating an ex of one of your friends.

Jalus and I began talking, and then began dating. He was great and I felt so happy with him. Celest and Riz had mentioned to me though that they had heard Jalus had badly beaten his ex-girlfriend. But I was never one to judge people and he treated me so nicely. I was nineteen and Jalus was twenty-two. We were happy all the time, drinking, going out and just enjoying every minute with each other. He made me feel so happy. Celest and Sy would always hang out with us. It was fun having Celest and I dating cousins because we always got to hang out. My parents watched my daughter all the time and I was trying my best to not scare Jalus with the fact that I had a daughter. I wanted him to ease in to being a father figure for my daughter. I was all in my flesh though and we loved having wild sex after a night of partying.

However, it wasn't too long before I began getting real feelings of love for Jalus. I mean, like he meant everything to me. Ty had found out about Jalus and me one day. Ty showed up when Jalus and I were walking out. Ty just stood there in shock, but I was in love with Jalus. Jalus and Ty had words when Ty kept texting my phone one night. I showed Jalus how much I loved him and hated Ty. I made Jalus text Ty because he was blowing up my phone with calls and texts.

Jalus sent a text saying, "She is mine now and I am going to screw her for you." I enjoyed knowing that Ty was going to be suffering and hurt.

I loved Jalus more than anything in this world. Two months after Jalus and I were dating, Liza called his phone. It came out that she was just testing me when she gave me the ok to date Jalus. I thought that was totally stupid. I mean, I am a very real and straight up kind of person. I do not ever expect one of my friends to test me. Just be real, be straight up. So Liza and I were no longer friends, but I still had Jalus. He and I were head over heels for each other. We loved getting our haters mad just by showing them how in love with each other we were.

One night, however, our relationship took a very strange turn. It was about four months from the day we started dating. I told Jalus, "Baby, I am going to take a shower." We were in my room at my parents' house. Jalus and I spent every day and night with each other since we began dating.

Jalus said, "All right, Sweetness, just do me a favor and leave the water on. I do not want your parents to know that I am bathing here."

I thought he was joking. "Ok, Jalus, but you know my parents don't care." I laughed and went into the bathroom. I showered and got out. I walked out of my bathroom to Jalus sitting on my bed. Jalus looked different. His eyes looked like he was no longer there.

I began kissing Jalus and then he said, "You did not leave on the water." Then he slapped me.

I said, "Jalus, what is all this about? I thought you were joking when you said that."

Jalus then stood up and slapped me to the ground. I could not believe what had just happened. I was totally confused. This was not like Jalus. He ended up apologizing after we smoked a spliff together. If only I had known that this was just the beginning.

After this Jalus began arguing with me over little things from the past. If someone got him upset, he would argue with me like it was my fault. He began relating everything his exes had done to him like it was me who had done the mean things to him. Then he started trying to convince me that I needed to confront his exes for what they did to him, like I was the one who needed to address what they did to him and make them pay. I did not understand why Jalus wanted me to act like this with girls I had no problems with. But he would say, "So you are taking their side then? I knew you didn't love me!" In my heart, I felt like maybe, just maybe, if I showed Jalus love it would soften his heart. I mean, Jalus was who my Daughter knew as "Daddy." I wanted it to work out with us for her sake.

Jalus and I always went out every weekend and even if we fought all that day, we would put on a show like we were so in love. Jalus had not hit me since that one time, but it all changed on my daughters first birthday.

My daughter and I were at Jalus' house. Jalus lived with his family. I was talking to Jalus and he got very mad about the fact that I was always honest with him when a guy hit on me while I was out. I told him because I did not want to make him feel like I was hiding it from him. But Jalus did not respect the fact that I was honest with him, it would always become a trick question with him. He had asked that night, "So, Baby, did any guys hit on you while you were out?"

I responded, "Yes, Jalus, but I told them I had a wonderful man at home." In a normal relationship the guy would have kissed his girlfriend and admire the fact that his girlfriend stuck up for their relationship.

Unfortunately, this would be the point I would find out Jalus and I had nothing close to a normal relationship. Jalus then said, "Oh, really? So, you like guys hitting on you awa?"

"Jalus, come on. Let's not argue. Let's enjoy Lilly's birthday." She was playing in the living room by the television.

All of a sudden he said, "So, you like trying to make me feel jealous or what, Bitch?" Then all I saw was a iron pot being thrown at me. It struck my arm and fell next to my daughter. I dropped down in severe pain, grabbing my arm and crying. Jalus ran up and kicked me five times as hard as he could on my sides and my legs. I could barley move once he was done kicking.

Then he said, "Is that what you like?" I was so confused. I did not understand how the man that once made me feel happier than any other man could suddenly turn.

It became very confusing. He would say he wanted someone without a kid. He would tell me that if I changed certain things about myself then he and I would get along better. He said that's why I had so many failed relationships. It was because of how I acted, even though Jalus never knew the details. Now when it came to him apologizing, it started becoming very confusing. He would say he did not mean anything and he was sorry, and if he hit me he would promise never to do it again. If I had a bruise from him beating me, he would turn it around, play the victim and make it my fault because people looked at him badly. He would blame me for what his ex-girlfriends had done and I wanted so desperately to prove him wrong.

Jalus believed that because he didn't have money that he could not be loved, but I told him all the time, "Baby, I just want you to love me and treat me good." He would make it seem like he understood, but it would come right back on me not even a week later, every time.

It started getting a lot worse. He became so paranoid and told me to call him every hour if I was at work. He also said that I could not hang out with my friends alone anymore because he just knew I was talking about him. Jalus would always tell me, "You see most men would not want to be with a woman with a kid. You're lucky I accepted you." He then began always condemning me about my past and who I use to be.

That was so messed up, though, because I never judged Jalus for his past. He had told me about him robbing places, dealing drugs, and abusing one of his ex-girlfriends. I still loved him. I felt that as a Christian, I should forgive Jalus for everything he did. I felt like maybe if he saw how much I forgave and loved him that he would be able to turn back into that Jalus that I first met. I told Jalus at one point that I wanted to tell my testimony and do something for God.

Jalus said, "I refuse to be with you if you ever tell your story." I told him that I wanted to someday minister to people in prison and that I prayed for God to open a door so that I could. Well, Jalus was not for that idea either. Jalus blamed me for everything in my past including my rapes. He said, "You should have fought them off harder."

If I ever hung out with Celest or Riz alone I could only stop by there house for ten minutes when I got off of work. Even my family became an enemy to Jalus. I always had to be on a time limit with him. Jalus always believed I was telling people about him abusing me to make him look bad. I never did tell anyone. As a matter of fact, I played it off like we were the happiest couple ever. I guess I accepted all of this behavior because he made me feel like that was the best I deserved for who I use to be.

It was almost like it had become a sick game he would play with my mind. He would tell me things he hated about me and what I needed to change, then afterwards I would burst into tears and cry myself to sleep. He would tell me the next morning that he did not mean anything he said. However, just as soon as I forgave him and forgot all about it, he would start all over again. I made a list once on all the things I needed to do to make Jalus happy.

My mother found the list and asked me, "What are you doing to yourself?" My parents always tried to help me, but I always pushed them away.

About a year and three months into our relationship the physical, emotional and mental abuse went to a whole new level. Jalus began threatening my mother, and thought everyone was out to get him and make him look bad. Most of the time, he thought even his closest friends were against him. I became the main target, however, so I hardly brought my daughter around anymore because it was too dangerous. Jalus would sometimes seem like he had changed, but the moment I would let my guard down, all hell would break loose. Jalus was a very insecure person, so I began praying for him. That's how much I loved Jalus and how much I wanted him to love God too. I wanted Jalus to live a life free from worrying about what people thought of him. Jalus was on probation and could not land a stable job and every time something went wrong, he would lash out at me. Regardless of how much I bought him, how much I loved him, if Jalus did not do it by himself, or get it for himself then it did not matter to him.

One night I was lying in bed with Jalus when all of a sudden I heard him screaming at me saying, "I am going to beat the hell out of you, Bitch!"

I jumped up in bed and looked at Jalus. He was asleep and nothing was coming out of his mouth. Then suddenly as I went to wake Jalus up, I felt a presence cover my mouth. I was trying to speak, but I couldn't get the words out of my mouth.

Then Jalus was shaking me. I thought it must have been a dream, but then Jalus said, "What was wrong with you, Babe? You were trying to talk but nothing was coming out." I remember feeling the chills go down my spine. I felt maybe Jalus was so different that maybe I was actually dealing with a demon. Now you may be thinking, *why didn't you just leave him?* Well, Jalus made it seem like no one liked him and I felt sorry for him. He was abused as a child and he had to watch his mother be abused by his father. I just felt like maybe I could show him love. Real love. I mean, Jalus did treat me nice at times, but the minute something did not go his way then everything fell apart. That sweet Jalus became enraged with anger.

Jalus and I had begun working for my parents, but that did not last long at all. Jalus and I both quit. Jalus came up with an idea.

He said, "Baby, I have an idea on how we are going to make tons of money." At the time, Jalus and I were both major potheads. That was one of the main things that Jalus loved about me. I was a tattooed, white girl that loved weed. He went on to explain, "Baby, you have tons of friends that smoke weed and so do I. So, let's sell it." At first I was totally against this, but when Jalus had an idea I truly had no say in what I thought. It was either his way or I had hell to pay. Either I go along or there was an argument till 4:00 a.m on how I was always against his ideas.

So we bought a pound and a half of weed. We were planning on moving into my parents' apartment. We sold about $400 worth and we decided to go shopping to get food for our new apartment. We still had a decent amount of weed in my dashboard. We went to leave from the grocery market and then I looked in my rear view mirrors. All I saw was red and blue lights.

I shouted, "Oh, my God, Jalus, we are going to go to jail!" I began having an anxiety attack, I could not breathe.

Jalus said, "Oh, hush, Babe!" He flung a bag of some of the weed out of the car. I had to pull over immediately because the police were demanding us to. I pulled over and sure enough they found the weed. Jalus and I both knew someone had given the police a lead.

Suddenly, the police put Jalus and I in handcuffs. Jalus let his anger take over. The police did not like Jalus either. The police dealt with Jalus horribly. They kicked him while he was handcuffed and slammed his foot in the door of the cruiser. I was just worried about Jalus, so I did the unthinkable and told the police that the weed was mine. I wanted Jalus to see how much I loved him. Well, he and I went to court and we were both sent to prison. I went for a week and Jalus went for two weeks. I used my time in prison to minister to the women in there. I missed Jalus terribly and he missed me.

My parents brought my daughter to prison to see me. I have never felt more horrible in my life, knowing I could not go home with my daughter. The week finally passed; the judge put me on probation in drug court for a year. Which meant I could not smoke weed any more. While I waited for Jalus to be released from prison for that week I was out, I did not eat or sleep. I was so in love with Jalus. I believed that after what I had done for him that maybe Jalus would see how much I loved him. I prepared the apartment for us. I worked as hard as I could for that week, making money so Jalus could have a lawyer. I even took my daughter to see Jalus in prison. Jalus looked like he missed us so much.

He said, "Baby, everything is going to be different when I get out." When Jalus was released, we had the best make up sex ever that night, and we both slept so peacefully.

Celest and Sy had come over that night and we were all smoking. I was scared so I took just one hit, and I was afraid I was going to be sent back to prison. You see, if I was caught with a dirty urine test I would be sent back to prison. Jalus had an awesome lawyer that got him off with no drug court, just a year more of his probation.

Needless to say, not too long after Jalus got out the arguments started happening again. Jalus then said, "I liked you better when you smoked weed." Which made me feel horrible because I couldn't smoke. Jalus would smoke in the apartment sometimes, which got me very upset. I did not want to have a dirty urine test from second hand inhalation. I was also upset because he disregarded what I had done for him.

One day Jalus said, "Baby, I want us to move back to my mothers," I just had to agree as usual with no say in anything.

He would say, "Baby, if we moved there then I would be happy and we would not argue." I believed every word. He always gave me hope.

One day an argument sparked with Jalus over my daughter. He started saying I was trying to show him up on the fact that she was not his biological daughter. Everything I did became offensive to him. It was very odd because he would act like a father to my daughter, but then sometimes practically anything would set him off.

I asked him one day, "What is this about now?"

He answered, "You know what the hell you are doing."

I responded, "Jalus I am just trying to be a good mom to Lilly. Why do you take offense if my attention is turned to her for even a minute?"

Next thing I know Jalus began punching me in my face and head. I screamed as loud as I could in pain, which made Jalus angrier. He began kicking and stomping me like he was fighting a man his size.

Honestly, Jalus was the one I could not fight back. You see, when you truly love someone and give your heart to him or her, you won't fight back. I did not hate him or want to hurt him, not that I would have a chance to because Jalus was full of muscles and almost a foot taller than I was. I also feared if I fought back the punches would get harder and he was already hitting hard enough.

My whole body was bruised. Jalus yelled, "Get out of my house with your stupid kid." He picked up my bloodied and bruised body and literally threw me out of his house. He then shouted, "I am going to have a new girl in my bed by tonight."

I grabbed Lilly, crying and jumped in my car. I never said anything mean to Jalus, I was too afraid.

I arrived at my parents' house beaten and bruised and heartbroken as well. I did not understand. I prayed all the time for Jalus, even more than I prayed for myself. My parents were furious when they saw me and how bloodied and beaten I was. No one had known Jalus was abusing me. My self-esteem and self-worth was nothing anymore. I had truly given Jalus my heart and he broke it with total disregard.

A little while later I heard a car pull up. I thought is it Jalus coming to say he was sorry. I ran down the stairs and opened the door to see Jalus had thrown my clothes all over my parents' yard. I was devastated to know I meant so little to him when I had made him my everything. So I did what I always had known to do when I could not handle life. Forget about it and go back to my flesh.

I began talking to Dale for about three days after Jalus and I had broken up. I began drinking and popping pills like they were Skittles. I wanted to numb the heartbreak and all of the hurt. The problem was that when you actually fall in love with your heart, you cannot get out of it with your flesh.

Dale had changed since we had last seen each other. Kate had died in car accident, pregnant with his child. I could see he was deeply affected by it. Dale tried to get my mind off of Jalus, but for some reason I could not shake the thought of him. He was my whole heart. On the fourth night of talking with Dale, he and I got drunk. But something went terribly wrong. Dale and I got into an argument and for the first time he hit me. This was not just a normal hit. Dale punched me over and over again in my face. I felt my face on fire, and it was drenched in blood.

I screamed, "Stop! What are you doing?" The blows kept coming and I felt my body giving out.

He dragged me out of my car, kicking, choking and punching me. I began to inhale my own blood. The hits just kept coming and suddenly I knew I was dying.

Dale said, "I'm going to kill you and everyone is going to think it was Jalus." Dale began trying to twist my neck so it would break.

I screamed, "Please do not kill me. I have a daughter!" Suddenly, the pain of him punching me over and over again stopped. Everything around me went into slow motion. You know you are about to die when that begins to happen. I saw my daughter, except she was older. She was asking my cousin, Rose, about me. She was saying how much she missed me.

Dale tried to kill me for six hours straight. He kept beating me and trying to break my neck.

I remember looking at the moon and saying, "God, please. I beg you, don't let me die." Then a miracle happened; Dale suddenly let me go. The next day I told Dale in a text not to ever come around me again. I was twenty years old and my life was almost taken from me.

But I did not acknowledge the fact that God delivered me from being killed. I was afraid and alone. I went back to Jalus thinking I would be safe, but a week after Jalus and I were back together, living in his mother's apartment, it all began again.

He said, "I want to know everything that happened between you and Dale." I began telling him, but he had his own truth he wanted to hear. The questions became more aggressive. Jalus picked up a knife and held it to my throat. The truth I was telling him, he did not want to accept. Jalus wanted the truth that made sense to him. So I lied and gave Jalus the story he wanted to hear. He was living in a different world, a world in which he webbed everything from his past and mine into the present.

Jalus began beating me up every week, for the situation with Dale. He would say, "If you really want to be my woman, you would act like this." He would tell me things I needed to change, like not being so funny all the time. Jalus said, "Do not ever tell Riz or Celest what I say to you. You are not tell anyone. No one will understand the terms we are on."

So I began living a lie and whenever Celest or Riz would call I would say, "Oh Jalus is so great. He is just so sweet." Most of the time Jalus would have them on speaker. I would always pray "God, please do not let Celest or Riz bring up anything about one of my exes." Jalus would beat me up if they ever mentioned something even remotely related to one of my exes. I hardly called Celest or Riz around Jalus anymore. I would wait till I was at work.

Every time after Jalus would beat me up he would say, "Baby, the truth is, if I had money then we would be happy and I wouldn't be so angry." Or "Baby, if I had a car then I would be happy." It got to the point that if he got something he wanted then the abuse would stop or so he made it seem. So I would think maybe when he had all these things he will be happy. That little bit of hope was what I clung to. Jalus would always tell me that no one would ever love me like he did and that most men would not accept me.

I believed that maybe if I got him saved and into the things of God that he would change. So I stayed and that was one big mistake I made. I was condemned and beat all the time. It became so bad that I was not allowed to wear certain colors anymore, not even certain hairstyles. He would relate practically anything to my exes and say, "You know what you are doing." Jalus always said, "I am different because I never cheated on you, so you should be happy."

One day Jalus was at this school program that he was going to. Lilly and I went and picked him up. Jalus kissed me and said hi to Lilly. I was taking Jalus to his probation officer because he had an appointment. Well, I began telling Jalus on the drive there how much I hated this girl named Kate. Well, of course, Jalus related that Kate to Dale's Kate that had died.

Jalus said, "You always bring up Dale."

I replied, "Jalus, just because someone I do not like has the same name as Dale's old girlfriend that died that is not relating everything to Dale." Then I made the mistake of saying, "Jalus, you are crazy sometimes. How does everything relate to everyone in the past?" Suddenly, there was that look, and I knew what was coming next.

Jalus then delivered a hard punch to my face. My car swerved in the road and I screamed, "Are you crazy?" That made him punch me nonstop. I almost lost control of my car. I pulled over and the beating continued.

Finally, it was done and Jalus said, "You know better." I looked at Lilly in the back seat and saw the look of fear on her face.

Jalus apologized later that day saying, "I do not mean to get so mad, but I feel like whenever you even mention someone's name that relates to Dale, you are trying to be spiteful."

Now whenever I talked to Jalus I had to second-guess everything I was going to say and how Jalus could possibly relate it to anything that would cause him to hit me. I had to be very careful, which was hard because I have always been a very talkative person. He then began saying whenever Lilly was around that he hated how her father had something over him. "If you got pregnant for me then I would be happy. I would know you are officially mine." Jalus began having sex with me every night to get me pregnant. It was totally messed up though. If Jalus had abused me or argued with me, the only way to stop the abuse or argument was to have sex. Jalus would say "Do not have sex with me if you feel bad." But I knew if I didn't the abuse and argument would continue.

Chapter Five

"Never forget that walking away from something unhealthy is BRAVE even if you stumble a little on your way out the door."

–Mandy Hale

I began crying to God every night saying, "God, please let Jalus see how much I love him and let him stop hurting me. I am so tired." Well, after two months, I got pregnant. Jalus was overjoyed and happy. Personally I was scared. I always told everyone I did not want to get pregnant again. However, to make Jalus happy I did. I was sicker than ever and could barely hold down any food. I was still working for my parents everyday. Jalus stayed at our apartment cleaning and relaxing.

One day when I was around three months pregnant, Jalus said, "Just keep talking, Bitch."

I asked, "What are you talking about, Jalus?" I had no idea what he meant. I was sitting on our couch eating some food while Jalus was in the bathroom.

Jalus replied angrily, "I hear you saying shit about me." I had not said a thing and I was totally confused. I began crying and started walking to our room. Jalus was now in the kitchen and had bumped me in the hall while he was walking to the kitchen. Jalus grabbed the hot frying pan from the stove. Suddenly, when I went to turn into the room from the hall, I felt a hard stinging blow to my back. I fell down in severe pain. Through blurred vision I saw the frying pain lying next to me on the floor. I slowly got to my feet and stumbled to our room.

Hurting and crying, I curled up in our closet to pray. "God, please let him change."

About an hour later, after I had cried myself to sleep, Jalus came in the room. He lay down beside me on the bed and whispered, "Baby, I am sorry. I just really had a bad day. How are you feeling?"

In some twisted way I felt that forgiving Jalus was the godly thing to do, and I did not want to let Him down. I kept thinking God would change him. I never let anyone know he was abusing me, especially through my pregnancy. I thought if I smiled and covered it up Jalus would see how much I loved him.

Jalus always believed everyone knew he abused me, so he would be worried to even leave the house. Somehow he would always turn himself into the victim and make it seem like I made him do it. I had to prove to Jalus that no one knew, if someone asked about a bruise, which there always were and they were always huge, I would lie and make it seem like I had just been clumsy. At the time, Lilly lived with my parents, she only spent a couple nights occasionally with Jalus and I. I was so unsure of how safe it was having her around. I thought once the baby arrived then Jalus would change, but there was always some new obstacle.

Jalus stopped abusing me for a couple of months. We were actually happy and praying together a lot. Then one day he was informed that the school that had promised him a job would not be giving him one. The abuse started up again. He would punch me in the face for anything and everything. He even broke a chair on me. I was now seven months pregnant. Jalus was verbally abusing me as well as physically abusing me. It was all the time now and I was getting so stressed out. I told him one day I was leaving. I just could not take him yelling at me anymore.

I began walking out of the apartment and opened the door. Jalus said, "Do not ever come back, Bitch."

I hollered back, "Fine! I won't Jalus." I was crying. As I went to step down our steps, Jalus kicked me in the middle of my back and I fell down the stairs, slamming into my car that was parked at the bottom of them. I landed on my side, holding my stomach with our son inside. Jalus came down the stairs and began kicking and punching me all over while I was on the ground. I screamed out, "Think about our son, Jalus."

He screamed, "I hope it dies!" Jalus then began stomping and punching my stomach. I was trying my best to cover my stomach from the blows.

I cried out, "Jesus, save me and my son." All a sudden Jalus's big brother Zalan ran out and grabbed him.

Zalan hollered, "What the hell are you doing? That is your son in there!"

I was in a great deal of pain. I struggled to get up. Zalan led me into their mother's house. He helped me into the house and onto the couch and asked, "Are you ok? Do you need to go to the hospital?"

I cried, "No, I just want to go to my parents."

Zalan led me back out to my car, making sure Jalus would not run out of our apartment and have another go at me. I drove off crying asking, "God, how can you let this happen to me?"

I arrived at my parent's house after trying to pull myself together. I just told them I was just stopping by to visit. I covered up how much pain I was in and walked into my old bedroom. I laid myself down on the bed and realized my son was not moving in my stomach. My stomach felt stiff, I prayed, "Oh, God, please let my son move and then I said to my son in my stomach, "I speak life to you in the Name of Jesus." All of a sudden, he started kicking me stronger than ever. I took a deep breath in relief knowing my son was alive. I just lay on my bed thinking no one even knows what pain I am going through in this pregnancy. I felt stuck in the very situation I was running from, but I was so in love with Jalus. All I could think of was the little bit of good times we had and maybe, just maybe, God would change him.

I felt so ashamed being abused again, and now this time by a man that I was actually in love with. Jalus would tell me all the time that it was my fault and I caused him to be like he was. He would constantly bring up the past. The truth to it is that Jalus could not let his past go and the person he became.

About an hour later, I called Riz and asked, "Hun, do you mind if I come over?"

She answered, "Yeah, Mama, come on over."

I was still in a lot of pain, but in denial of what had just happened. I needed to smoke some weed. I did not want to go to a hospital, I just wanted to be around one of my best friends that loved me and made me laugh. So I changed my clothes and walked out the door of my parent's house only to find Jalus by my car.

Jalus looked at me in sympathy and said, "Baby, I am so sorry I lost my temper. I do not know what I was thinking."

I simply replied, "Jalus, just get in the car. I do not want to talk at my parent's house."

"Where are we going?"

"To Riz's house."

"I think you should go to the hospital."

His reply nauseated me. He had no concern when he was trying to kill our son in my stomach, but suddenly now he did? Jalus asked the question he always asked after he beat me up, "So, Baby, did you tell anyone what happened?"

"No Jalus!" I responded angrily. My mind was racing all the way to Riz's house. I contemplated what I was going to do about Jalus and I. I just felt like I had one kid already and about to have two. How was I going to raise them by myself? It seemed impossible. We arrived at Riz's and, as always, I acted like nothing had happened and lied about how good he was treating me.

Time passed and I was 8 months pregnant. Jalus and I were living in my parent's apartment. My family and Jalus had stopped talking from the time Jalus and I had broke up before I was pregnant after he beat me up. But I convinced my family he had changed and was treating me nicely. I wanted them to be all right with each other, considering I was pregnant with his son. My family had no idea, though, that Jalus was abusing me throughout the entire pregnancy.

It wasn't long before Jalus started screaming and fighting about the simplest things. If I bought food for us and did not eat with Jalus he would say, "Now you showing me face about food!" It was always something and whenever Jalus got angry I could sense the presence of it before the argument even started. Jalus's face would totally change and his eyes looked like there was no soul in them, only hatred. As arguments escalated I learned to never argue with him. I was just quite and would find a place to cry.

Once Jalus brought up the past again and hit me as hard as he could in my leg with a Mystic Bottle. If you have no idea what that is, it is a large thick glass bottle. The glass did not break, which hurt worse. I had a huge bruise on my leg about the size of a melon. I was going to wear shorts one day, but the bruise was still there and Jalus yelled, "You are going to wear shorts? You just love showing people your bruises, don't you?"

I always had to cover my bruises or he would give me another one to takes its place for embarrassing him. I don't know why, but I loved Jalus so much. He kept saying, "If I had this or that then I would be happy." I got him everything he wanted, hoping that maybe that would be the last obstacle for him. Somehow, Satan had twisted my thoughts into thinking Jalus would change if I just stayed with him. The thought of another girl being with him after I left was unbearable. After all, what if he DID change?

Two weeks before I was going to have my son, which I was scheduled to have by C-section because I was too small to have children normally, I was feeling depressed because I wanted to experience actual child birth. However, there was nothing I could do about it. Jalus started an argument with over the fact that I was moody, which being nine months pregnant I thought that was normal.

Well, Jalus didn't agree. "You act like this because you like to make me feel jealous about your ex-boyfriends!"

"No, Jalus, they are part of my past! Why do you always bring them up? What do they have to do with anything?"

Jalus lunged at me. I went to turn around and run, but being nine months pregnant your balance is not always good.

Besides that you can't move very fast. I turned around so quickly I hit my stomach against the bathroom door.

"You trying to kill my son, Bitch?" Jalus grabbed me and threw me to the bathroom floor and began punching me in the face and head, kicking me all over.

I screamed, "Jalus, please stop! You're hurting me!" But he didn't stop for a very long time. After I laid there curled up on the floor in a massive amount of pain, I prayed, "God, please show him what he is doing. Let him change, please!"

Finally, I was able to walk over to my parents' house. Jalus was outside. I had cleaned myself up, of course, and lay down in my bed. I was hoping Jalus would go get high and come back down from his enraged state.

Suddenly, I heard a knock on my door, "Honey, it's Dad." I opened my door and Jalus was standing there with both of my parents. Dad said, "We all need to talk."

Jalus had come over and admitted to my parents that he hit me. I know what a shock it was to my parents. I had kept it hidden from them. We talked for over an hour. My dad counseled Jalus and I and admonished Jalus saying, "There will be no more hitting. None at all! These kids need a stable home. Jalus, I am trusting you never to hit my daughter again. Do you understand me?"

Jalus nodded his head and made it seem like this was the first time he hit me and I, of course, did not say anything about the rest of the abuse. I never understood why Jalus held anything from my past against me, but I never brought up how much abuse and pain he caused me. I loved him too much to even hold a grudge.

At times Jalus was so sweet and gentle. That's what I held onto during all of the abuse. Those rare, wonderfully nice moments helped blot out the pain of the abuse. From that moment on, every time Jalus would start an argument I would get my dad. He would sit and talk with Jalus for hours, sometimes into the early morning, just to help Jalus clear his head and thoughts. Deep down I knew my dad was not doing this for Jalus, but for the kids and me. He knew how much I loved Jalus. Just a few nights before I was suppose to go into the hospital, an argument escalated regarding a color I wore.

"That is that pussy's color," He said referring to Dale. I tried to go for my dad, but Jalus stopped me at the door. "You going tell your parents again, little bate?" which in English means tattle tale.

I cried, "Jalus, just stop! Ok?"

Jalus's eyes began to change again. Jalus was without a soul once again. I closed my eyes and knew what was coming next. Punch after punch, I screamed. After Jalus was finished beating me, he went outside to smoke some weed. As usual, I went into the bathroom to look in the mirror and the damage. I felt my head. I had lumps all over and noticed bruises behind my ears on my head. This time, however, the backs of my earrings were lodged into my head. I was scared seeing the bar of the earrings fully stuck to my head. I pulled them out and blood trickled down my neck. I knew I needed to get my parents. I couldn't take another beating that night if Jalus didn't calm down. So I ran across the street to my parent's house. It was 2:00 in the morning. I banged on their door, but there was no answer. Everyone was sound asleep. When I ran to my parent's, Jalus was behind our apartment, smoking weed. I kept banging on my parents' door, but they had an upstairs apartment. Suddenly, I saw Jalus walking across the street with his eyes filled with hate. My heart was pounding out of my chest and my son was kicking in my stomach.

"What the hell are you doing?"

"Nothing," I stuttered.

"You're going tell your parents? Well, tell them this!" he shouted and delivered three hard right hooks to my forehead, leaving me dizzy and disoriented. "Now get your ass back in our apartment."

I did just what he said. "Please, just don't hit me anymore," I begged. Jalus shoved me while I was walking over to our apartment.

I ran into our bedroom, but caught a glimpse of myself in the bedroom mirror. I had a huge lump on my forehead. One of those lumps you see cartoon characters have after getting hit with a hammer. I could not believe what I saw in the mirror. At the same moment Jalus walked up with some ice and said, "Lay down." Jalus held the ice on my forehead. I remember looking at his hands thinking those same hands taking care of me are the same hands that hurt me. Jalus gave the same apology, "Baby, I love you and I promise I will never do this again."

The next morning I had to go over to my parent's house to get my laundry. The minute my dad opened the door his face was saddened, but I did what I always did best made up a story to cover for Jalus. "Oh, Dad, an iron fell on my head." That little laugh I gave off, that laugh was saying I wish I could tell someone. Jalus made me feel so bad for him like he was the one that had to cover up everything and the bruises. It was always my fault to Jalus. Now, even though my dad counseled Jalus, he never really explained how farfetched his thoughts were. I guess Jalus knew deep down it was insane to relate everything to the past like a web. But I never told anyone that even a certain color could set Jalus off. I had finally started teaching myself how to survive in the world of Jalus, where anything and everything could relate to the past. I learned how to walk on eggshells for my safety. Jalus made sure that I always believed no one would want me and that he was the best I was ever going to have.

Two days had gone by and I still had a lump with now a huge bruise right on my forehead. I had a doctor's appointment to discuss the C-section. Jalus was very demanding that morning while I was getting ready. I was in the bathroom trying to put on my makeup and cover the bruise that was black, blue and yellow. Jalus walked up to the side of me looking in the mirror.

"Can't you cover that better? Do you want people to know?"

I burst into tears. "I should not have to be doing this, Jalus."

All of a sudden Jalus turned very pale, like he had seen a ghost. Considering Jalus was dark skinned, he had looked very pale compared to his normal color.

"What happened to you just now, Jalus?"

He replied in a timid voice, "I was watching you do your make up in the mirror and you crying after you told me you shouldn't have to be doing this, but then I heard your voice say, 'Yeah, pussy!' However, your lips did not move in the mirror." Immediately I felt chills go up my spine, I thought could this be real? I wondered if possibly a demon was imitating my voice. This made perfect sense. All the times Jalus swore I was saying means things and I wasn't. I suddenly believed this was the result of a demon mimicking my voice and tormenting Jalus in his mind.

I told my parents about it and they said, "We need to pray."

The next day I went to the hospital to have my son. For the first time in a long time Jalus was overjoyed and full of life. For the three days my son and I were in the hospital that loving joyous spirit Jalus had continued. It's like the Jalus I first met was back. He was so loving towards me and happy to be with our son.

On the third day I was released to go home with our son. Jalus picked us up from the hospital and we stopped for food. Jalus kept showing people our son. I had named our precious son, Israel. We got home and because I had a C-section I could barely move, nonetheless pull my pants up. So much as a slight sneeze was complete agony. Jalus had cleaned our apartment beautifully. That night Israel was a bit fussy, I could not get Israel to latch on to my breast. While I was trying to feed Israel Jalus was outside smoking weed.

Israel was crying like most newborns do when, like a tornado, Jalus came running into the house screaming, "What are you doing to him?"

I was sitting on our bed trying to keep Israel warm and trying to comfort him so he could latch on. I responded by asking, "What are you talking about?"

"Keep it up, Bitch! Keep messing with my son! Why is he crying, huh?" He rushed at me with a fisted hand, "Put him down!"

I was terrified. I could not believe what was happening, but I did as I was told. I lay my son in his crib. The moment I did and turned around, Jalus slapped me as hard as he could in my face. I fell on the bed in severe pain. Not only did my face hurt, but the pain in my stomach was excruciating. I felt like my stitches popped open.

"The next time you do this I am going to pound you even worse," Jalus shouted sternly.

I cried harder than ever and was literally petrified of Jalus. He began pacing through the house muttering, "I should mess you up worse." While he was out of the room I dialed my mother's number and even though I could not say anything or Jalus would hear me, I left the phone connected, lying on the bed. I prayed that my mother would hear Jalus ranting.

Suddenly, Jalus busted through door again, and delivered three more blows to my head and told me to shut up. I was screaming loudly in pain and fear. Almost immediately there was a loud knock on our door. Jalus looked at me in rage and I ran straight for that door and opened it. It was my parents. I ran straight into my father's arms. My mother ran into my apartment like a mother hen protecting her chicks.

She began yelling at Jalus, "My daughter just had surgery and she just had your son and you treat her like this?" She pushed past Jalus and picked up Israel. My parents took Israel and I across the road to their house. My dad stayed with Jalus and talked to him for over two hours. I can't tell you what was said, but after that Jalus came over with him with a so-called "sincere" apology.

I would love to say the abuse stopped, but it didn't and now I was stuck covering for Jalus again. He would now beat me if I missed buttoning a button on my son's clothes. He would even beat me if my son's shirt was put on backwards. I eventually stopped breast feeding my son because I would be beaten all the time if I could not get my son to latch on to my breast. I felt nervous every time I tried to breastfeed my son in front of him. My father counseled Jalus about every three days and of course I denied that Jalus was abusing me again. Jalus would always tell me, "I don't want your parents looking at me badly." I always thought maybe if Jalus saw how loving and close and forgiving my family was he would be a loving person as well, considering he never had a loving family as a child.

A couple of weeks later my parents announced they would be moving back to California. I was twenty-one now and the thought of being alone with Jalus was scary. I wanted to go with them, but then Jalus would not be able to go. Jalus was still on probation, and for some reason I still loved him. I was so worried that if I left Jalus he would kill someone or get himself killed with the temper he had. The thought to me was unbearable. I wanted to be there for him even if that meant sacrificing my happiness and my body.

My parents began closing all of their shops, and we started a garage sale. However, this was not your average garage sale. We were selling all the stuff that was in our shops and storage for the last ten years. Furniture, movies, games and anything else you could possibly imagine was displayed in front of our houses.

I became in charge of the sale. I was moving almost one to two hundred boxes of movies out each day, moving furniture and anything else. I had developed an eating disorder because of all the stress of being abused by Jalus. He would physically, emotionally and verbally abuse me. I would go for days sometimes without eating. I just felt worthless and thought maybe if I were skinnier and prettier then Jalus would love me.

Jalus found a new issue to be angry about. He wanted a car just to have before we left the island. I traded my car for another one and gave it to him. I even paid for the license and insurance. The day I did this I asked Jalus to watch our son so I could get it all done for him. I bought shoes that he wanted and asked him, "Hun, do you mind if for once I treat myself to getting my nails done with Riz?" I always had to ask permission. This was the first time I asked for time alone with one of my friends since we got together.

Jalus responded, "Yeah, I guess that's ok." I was thrilled! This was going to be actual girl time and I could just relax and enjoy myself with my dear friend.

Riz picked me up from the licensing department and we were already beginning to enjoy ourselves. We started getting our nails and toes done. I loved acrylic nails, which normally take a while. Riz and I were having a great time and one of our close guy friends Petey was there. He was one of Jalus's younger cousins. Then as we began to leave to go pick up some food my phone rang. It was my mother.

"Jalus just left here speeding in the car you bought for him. He had Israel in the front seat with no car seat!"

I almost dropped the phone when I heard. My son was only two months old. My face turned absolutely pale and Riz asked, "What's wrong, Ma?"

I explained to Riz what my mother just told me. Riz and Petey tried to calm me down and took me to get the food. I kept trying to call Jalus. When he finally answered I screamed at him, "What the hell are you thinking? Our son is only two months old!"

Jalus said, "I am coming to get you now. Why has it been taking so long just to get your nails done, huh?"

Riz and Petey saw my face turn into utter fear. I was afraid and confused. Jalus had told me to stay at the restaurant because he was almost there. Fifteen minutes later Jalus finally arrived in the car I just got him. Even though I was scared of Jalus, I was even more angry. I was angry that he would be so careless with our son and that I was always beaten for things that were not even close to being a threat to our son, like putting a shirt on backwards. It disturbed me that Jalus thought he could get away with stuff like this and the truth. But the truth was he always could because I was a woman and I was smaller. Jalus greeted Riz and Petey and I just looked at him knowing this all was just an act for Riz and Petey, like Jalus was totally cool with everything and just wanted to say hello.

I gave Jalus the shoes I got him and then a guy walked by that Jalus knew. "Hey, Jalus, those are nice shoes man, you selling them?"

"Yeah, man, how much would you give me for them?"

I became very angry and grabbed the shoes, "Why you always act like everything I give you is not worth anything to you?" Jalus just chuckled. "And how could you be so careless with Israel?"

"Get in the car. We are going home."

I knew if I got in the car with Jalus the cool act he had going would change and he would beat me up all the way home.

"No!" Then it escalated. Jalus grabbed me, but out of anger I started hitting his car with my shoes. "You got a car now, Jalus! What is the problem, huh?"

He started throwing me around like a rag doll. He eventually pushed me into the car, slapping my head against the door. Riz screamed, "Jalus, you do not have to handle her like that! She is just scared of you. That is why she does not want to go with you."

Riz witnessed how Jalus really was as I sat in the car. While Riz was talking to Jalus I saw her face that she was very concerned and worried. Then all of a sudden I saw red and blue lights, the police had been called by someone in the restaurant. I got out of the car and they began questioning Jalus and I. Riz was holding Israel when suddenly one of Bri's sisters pulled up with her boyfriend and asked what happened.

"This guy is putting me through hell," I cried.

Bri's sister had to leave, but she replied "Call me, Love."

The police questioned Jalus and I about what happened. Yes, I covered once again. But one of the police officers noticed marks on my face. Jalus and I where taken to the police station and then released. Once Jalus and I arrived home, my family confronted us. They were angry with Jalus and asked where his head was at when he took our two-month-old son into a car with no car seat, and why I could never have time alone with my friends. Petey and Riz were there as well. Jalus tried saying he had just missed me. My family accepted Jalus's apology and so did I. It wouldn't be long before my parents were going to be leaving the island.

I agreed with my parents that I would keep the sale going and send them money every week. Jalus, Israel and I were going to fly up to the States once we had enough money.

I remember the day my parents and brother where leaving. I let them take Lilly with them. My parents both talked to Jalus, making sure he would not hurt me and was changed. I knew differently, but yet I didn't say anything. I guess the thought of failing in the one relationship I really tried hard to make work wasn't an option in my book.

Chapter Six

"The most common way women give up their power is by thinking they don't have any."

–Alice Walker

As I watched my family drive off, I began to cry and Jalus said, "Don't worry, Baby, I will take care of you."

Well life was finally going good for a few days. Jalus and I watched over my parents' house and stayed there some nights. We always had money now and I ran the sale everyday from 8:00 a.m. to 10:00 p.m. Jalus tended to Israel. Even though I knew I wasn't supposed to be moving boxes and furniture after just having a C-section, I still pushed through. I bought Jalus anything he wanted; however, that was never good enough to make him happy unless he got it for himself. About four days after my family had left, the verbal abuse started again. He would say things like, "If I was off my probation and didn't have a probation officer then I would be happy. If only we were in the States then we would not argue."

I was so exhausted from trying to meet every need that he wanted to be happy. I thought about how unfair it was that I had to always be the strong one and the encourager. Just a week after my parents were gone, the physical abuse started again. I prayed to God all the time, but I just felt like God wasn't listening now. I questioned why He could not change Jalus.

Two days later, I was in the middle of a sale dealing with customers and Jalus was verbally bashing me. I went inside to get some change. I just felt like I was doing so much to make life good for him and he was so ungrateful. I wondered why I deserved this bad treatment. So I told Jalus, "You need to leave. I hate how you treat me all the time."

Now Jalus knew he could not hit me in front of all these people so he called his mother. She arrived but Jalus said, "I am taking Israel and we can work out time that you can have him."

I screamed, "Fine Jalus!" Then I noticed that $1,700 dollars of my money that I had worked for in the sale was gone. I hollered, "Give me the money back, Jalus, that is hard earned money." He just laughed and got in his mother's car.

Jalus and I were not on talking terms for two days. We began talking when I picked up my son from him. I am not going to lie. I felt very alone and missed our little broken family. Being in my parent's big house by myself at night was scary and I just felt so broken. I began drinking and smoking weed nonstop. Every time I saw Jalus he would try to kiss me and tell me he missed me. I still cared about Jalus so I brought him cigarettes and food and made sure he had diapers for Israel. I was so depressed, though, I honestly could not even run the sale. After a week since Jalus and I broke up I had spent a night or two at Celest's house because I needed some support and love. I went out to the bar by Jalus's house one night and I ordered five drinks for me.

Somebody told Celest I was out there with guys and was wasted and not wanting to take care of Israel. Celest called me yelling at me so I yelled back and said, "Celest, I thought you and I were cool."

She responded, "We are, Hun, just come by my house, ok?" So I kind of figured somebody had told her something incorrect.

Before I went there I saw Jalus out by the bar and Jalus said, "Are you coming back out here?"

I said, "Yeah, I think so, but I have to go see Celest first." I went to Celest's house and we talked and cleared things up. Then I got ready at Celest's house and headed back out to the bar that Jalus was at. I arrived and walked into the bar, but Jalus was nowhere in sight.

Then I received a text from Jalus saying, "I am going to the club with my boys since you did not come back."

I called Jalus, "What the hell are you talking about Jalus? I am out here now."

He just laughed, "Oh, ok, well come here." He was across the bar watching me the whole time.

Jalus and I started talking casually. We started drinking a lot as well. Both of us were pretty wasted and being really flirty with each other, even though we were not together. Then Jalus had received a call from his mom saying Israel was up. Jalus asked me if I wanted to come with him to put Israel back to sleep. So I did as any good mother would do. I remember putting Israel back to sleep and Jalus said, "I miss you, Sweetness." I just looked and Jalus and smiled. I knew deep down I missed him too, but I kept fighting it, knowing the abuse I would go back to. Once Israel was back asleep we left Jalus's house and went back to the bar. We had even more drinks, which left us both very intoxicated.

Jalus said, "Let's go to the club."

"I do not want to go to the club. We have enough issues with us. Let's just stay here."

"Come on. Let's go have a nice night."

After two more drinks I eventually said, "All right, fine, I will go."

Jalus told one of his guy friends named Grey to come with us. Grey was Kisha's child's father. Kisha was there as well and her friend Trini. So I drove my car to my parent's house and left it there. Jalus picked me up in his mother's car. We all began driving to the club. The club was on the west part of the island. It was about a twenty-minute drive from our district. We arrived at the club and it was packed. We all began drinking again. We were all dancing, just having a nice night. Jalus was being very sweet and kissing me while I was dancing with him. Grey and Kisha could not stop kissing each other either. However, like all good times it came to an end. The club was now closing.

I was ready to go home. Grey said, "Let's go to the after party." Eventually we found out where the after party for the night was being held. It was being held in Ty's district and neighborhood. Which, of course, I knew going there was a bad idea. But I did not want to tell Jalus we shouldn't go down there because of Ty. I knew how Jalus would get and would say I was bringing Ty up again. So I just went along with the plan.

We arrived and it actually seemed chill. We saw a lot of old friends. Everyone was smoking weed, listening to music and just having a good time. The after party was held in a parking lot behind a store. Jalus was very intoxicated now and so was I. I was getting pretty tired because it was now about 3:00 in the morning. Jalus and I decided to leave and began walking out of the party back to the car. All I could think about while walking back to the car was the abuse I had to go through and Jalus always making me feel like I was trying to show him a face about Ty. I wanted to prove my point to Jalus that Ty meant nothing to me, even though Jalus and I were still not together so I let it all out.

I said, "Jalus is a real man. He loves and takes care of me. He is such a good father." Yes, it was all a lie. I knew exactly how I was treated behind closed doors.

Deep down, I was venting all my anger of being abused. Then Ty's brother-in-law, Raul, saw me. Raul asked, "Are you talking to me or what?"

I just got angry and wondered, how would any of this relate to Raul? Raul knew I was making Ty look bad, but Raul was the type of person to take things personally. I sarcastically replied, "Who the cap fits!"

Jalus and I kept walking toward the car, which there were a lot of people around where the cars were parked. All of a sudden Ty was there. I began cursing at Ty for everything he put me through. All of the anger that had built up in me from what I was still going through just erupted. Suddenly, Jalus and Ty began arguing with each other. Soon Jalus and I were cussing out Raul and Ty. The whole crowd's attention was now focused on us and the argument was just escalating.

Jalus finally yelled, "Let's go forget these fools." Jalus and I jumped in the car. Ty was still arguing and yelling.

I stuck my head out the window and started telling Ty how much I hated him and how worthless he was. Then Jalus drove off.

Jalus was laughing and said, "Boy, you told Ty about his ass."

"Now do you understand how much I hate Ty?"

We were about five minutes up the road when Jalus said, "We should go back."

"Go back for what? There is nothing more to say."

"So you care about Ty or what?"

"Ok, Jalus, if that was not good enough for you, we will drive back across so you can be happy." Jalus seemed thrilled and turned the car around. I had a very weird feeling about this. It was like my spirit was saying, *Don't go*. Jalus pulled back up in front of the crowd and Ty was still there with Raul.

I stood up out of the window of the car and started telling Ty what a piece of shit dad he was. Jalus was smiling from ear to ear, of course. Ty started getting extremely angry. I had just given him the embarrassment of a lifetime and sat back down in my seat. Jalus looked over in time to see Ty hurl a glass bottle at my window. Lucky for me, Jalus saw it coming and had rolled my window up so that it didn't hit me. The moment this bottle hit I looked over at Jalus and all I saw was his back. Jalus took off out of the car running after Ty. I jumped out of the car running after Jalus. Just then I saw Jalus fly kick Ty straight to the ground.

I was trying to catch up to Jalus because he was a distance from me. For some reason Jalus was waiting for Ty to get up and fight him. I was about a good twenty feet away from Jalus when I saw Raul walking up behind Jalus with a pipe.

I hollered, "Jalus, watch out." Right when I said that, Raul swung at Jalus with the pipe. Raul was thinking he was going to catch Jalus in the head, but because I screamed and warned Jalus, it caught him in his mouth.

I ran as fast as I could towards Jalus. Raul thought the hit was going to knock Jalus out, but Jalus was fully conscience and tried to grab him. Raul ran and dropped the pipe in fear as I approached. Nothing looked wrong at first, but then Jalus started spitting out blood.

"We need to go now," Jalus hollered.

"I told you not to come back." Jalus and I walked back to the car and jumped in.

Jalus looked in his visor mirror and became enraged. "I'm going to kill them!" Jalus turned towards me and one of his teeth had gotten knocked out.

"Jalus, I told you I wanted to stay at the bar for this very reason."

"Just shut up! You watch what I am going to do."

Jalus began letting his anger build more and more on the drive back to his house. Jalus kept saying, "They are dead."

"Jalus, I want no part in this. Let me out by my parents house." We approached my parent's house, "Jalus let me out now!"

"No, you're coming with me!" Jalus yelled.

That sick feeling that something horrible was going to happen came over me. I just wanted to go home. I was so afraid when Jalus had that rage in his eyes. He was no longer there. Those eyes of rage that showed no soul.

We arrived at one of his cousin's house. Jalus ran straight into their house, waking up his cousins. I ran in the house to see what was happening. Jalus told his cousin, "Give me the gun. I need to deal with these pussies."

"No, Jalus, you need to think about this and calm down."

Jalus kept pacing back and forth. "If this happened to you, you know would blast them!"

I looked at his cousin, "Do not give Jalus a gun."

After about an hour Jalus convinced them to give it to him. His cousin walked outside and passed Jalus a loaded handgun. The minute I saw the gun I said "Screw this, I am going home. I will walk myself home."

I began walking off and Jalus ran up and grabbed my arm with the loaded gun in his hand. "You're coming with me!"

"Jalus, please! I do not want any part of this. Let me go home, please!" I begged with tears running down my cheeks.

Jalus pulled me towards the car. His cousins kept trying to convince Jalus to let me go, but Jalus did not want to hear it. He shoved me into the car and locked the door. We began driving. I remember crying and wondering what I was doing with a person like this. Even though we weren't together, I was deathly afraid of him still. I guess mainly because how bad the beatings were at times, but now I was actually afraid for my life. We finally arrived back in Ty's neighborhood except Jalus parked the car in an off road alley. This alley was about one hundred feet from where the incident took place. The sun was just started to arise, Jalus checked the gun to make sure it had six bullets.

I cried and said, "I am leaving." I tried to open the door to the car and get out, but Jalus immediately grabbed my arm and yanked me back into the car.

He looked at me with those eyes of rage and put the gun to my head. "I will kill you and then them, if you get out of this car." I could not believe that someone I loved so much and gave a son could possibly take my life.

Jalus then put the gun in his lap and wrapped his face with a shirt and jumped out of the car. I heard six loud shots. I prayed to God and said, "God, please let Jalus realize what he is doing and do not let anyone get killed. Oh, God, please help me." After I ended my prayer Jalus jumped in the car. I was scared and silent on the whole drive back. I just wanted to go home. I was terrified now of Jalus. I felt sick to my stomach and I just kept hearing those shots going off. I was too afraid to even ask Jalus if he killed anyone. I was honestly afraid of the answer.

Jalus finally broke the silence and said, "I didn't catch any of them, but they heard me. I know that for sure." I just remained quiet. Jalus was starting to sober up now. Right when Jalus arrived at my house, he began trying to kiss me and said how much he wanted to be with me.

I was still in shock of having a gun pointed at my head to be honest. But I loved him so much and knowing that he was hurt, I felt like I was supposed to take care of him. However, I had to ask Jalus one thing. "Are you going to blame me for you getting hurt and start beating me up again?"

"Oh, no, baby. I just want you to be here for me." So I went against that sick gut feeling that was saying, "You know he is never going to change."

I took care of Jalus for two weeks. I made special food for him so he could eat. I kept him totally out of pain with his jaw and mouth. I nursed him back to health and somehow could not shake the love I had for him. After the two weeks, the verbal abuse started up again and the same promise he made about not blaming me for him getting hurt. That promise was broken in no time just like all the other empty promises.

Then about three weeks after the incident occurred, Jalus and I were over by my parents place. We had to watch both places so we would go back and forth to make sure no one thought about trying to break in. Jalus started up again, this time about the incident between him, Ty and Raul. Jalus was saying because I talked to Lilly while she was in California with my parents, I was showing him Ty was better. I never understood half the time how Jalus related everything to Ty. I was trying my best to explain to Jalus that I just missed Lilly and wanted to talk to her. But those eyes appeared once again and I was in total fear the rage was back. I was trying my best to avoid getting Jalus angrier, but with Jalus he didn't need someone to argue with. He did not care how afraid and terrified I was of him. Israel was inside sleeping and somehow even though I was so afraid of Jalus, I was just happy my precious Israel was too young to witness and remember any of the abuse.

Then Jalus's anger took him over once again and I was the target. He came running at me full speed and I just closed my eyes and put my hands over my head. He delivered a great amount of hard blows to my face and head. He began dragging me by my hair and punching me in the face. He then kicked me and said, "Get up."

I got up shaking in so much pain and fear. I just looked up at the sky and quietly prayed, "God, help me please, so I do not have to feel any more pain." Then I saw a fist and everything went black. Jalus carried me into the house. I didn't understand what happened.

"What happened?"

"You passed out. I didn't knock you out." I knew Jalus must have knocked me out because the last thing I remember seeing was his fist coming at my face.

Jalus apologized once again for beating me up and gave me the same speech. "If we were in California, Baby, then I would be happy and not get mad at you."

About five days prior to us leaving the island Jalus began hearing voices again. I knew I would not be able to handle another beating.

I told Jalus, "Baby, You need to go get help. I will even pay for it. Just please go get help."

For once Jalus agreed that he needed help, so the next day I gave him $500 and he went to a psychologist. Jalus was diagnosed with Hyper Alertness and a slight case of Schizophrenia. Finally the day came that we were leaving for California. In my mind, I thought, *finally, a new life.* Jalus had told me if we were in California then he would be happy.

When we were on the plane Jalus started an argument once again about the past. I remember how embarrassing it was seeing how people were looking at us. After being with Jalus for so long I could never really become angry or at least show that I was angry. Voicing my opinion was totally out of the question. Finally, the plane rides were over and we landed in California. I was so happy to see my family and Lilly. Something in me felt like finally Jalus and I could have a new life.

The first couple of weeks went perfect. I was trying to get a job and Jalus was trying to make money online. Jalus started becoming depressed, though, about having to wait to get a green card and be able to work. I tried to encourage him all the time. I would take him out and try to show him life in California.

Then one day the first outburst after coming to the States happened. Jalus and I were getting ready for bed. That look appeared on Jalus's face once again.

I asked, "Baby, what's wrong?"

"Your family is trying to show me a face by using that color of plates to relate to Dale."

"Jalus, come on. Are you serious?" Then Jalus slapped me very hard across the face. I thought, *How is it that Jalus can still be like this?*

Jalus said, "You think because we are around your family that I have to put up with this." I just cried and went to sleep. In the middle of the night Jalus leaned over and said, "Baby, I am sorry." Then I felt his hand going up my thigh. I was required to have sex with him. If I did not, the argument would start back up and escalate. I try so hard and love him so much.

Jalus became depressed. He wanted to work. I had developed a severe eating disorder. I had lost about one hundred pounds in three months after I had Israel. I was even more stressed now trying to get a job so I could get Jalus his green card, so that he could work. Jalus would just sulk and not help out in the house or with the kids.

Except for Jalus being depressed all the time, he was staying pretty calm. One night all this changed and my family finally got to witness the true Jalus with those eyes of rage and no remorse. A fight escalated right in front of my mom, dad and my brother Seth. I was working at a full commission based job, which I had no idea would end up being a pyramid scheme. I walked door to door to different houses from 9:00 a.m. to 9:00 p.m. My body was exhausted all the time, but I knew if Jalus had his green card everything would be perfect like he said it would be. I came home late that night. I was so hungry and thirsty. I just wanted to go to sleep, but of course Jalus was upset with me. As usual, the past was brought up once again.

Jalus and I were in the living room and Jalus' yelling became louder and louder. My dad tried to calm him down, but Jalus was in that raging state that no one could calm. For once in my life I tried to get angry with Jalus. I snapped and I thought for one second I can be strong enough to defend myself. I let that anger build so much that when Jalus said what he did it pulled the trigger and my anger fired.

He said, "I wish we had never had Israel because you are so worthless."

I ran as fast as I could towards Jalus and fly-kicked him right in his chest. The minute I did that, Jalus punched me. My brother Seth rushed up to Jalus because he saw Jalus was trying to stomp on my face while I was on the ground. Seth delivered two hard punches to Jalus' face. Then Seth and Jalus were trying to cut off each other's air supplies. In the midst of all of that Jalus tried lunging at me. My mom, dad and brother all grabbed him and tried to hold him from getting to me. He even tried kicking my head and face, which my parents and brother saw him trying to do. They saw how serious Jalus was and realized the danger I was in. For once, I actually tried to fight back at Jalus. However, I was only five feet tall and much smaller than Jalus, so I did not achieve much damage. Besides that, the truth was that I did not want to hurt Jalus because I loved him too much. My father saw how much I loved Jalus, even though Jalus said and did the cruelest things. I had hope for him. So once again, my dad tried to counsel with him.

Some part of my heart could not let him go. I prayed for Jalus more than myself. Even though the physical abuse calmed down, the verbal and mental abuse would happen every couple of weeks. I could not even show my daughter love half the time because Jalus would say, "You need to love Israel first, then Lilly." I hated that I could not even be a good mom and I just felt so unwanted. I was trying my best, yet still I was yelled at and accused of not being good enough.

Jalus finally got saved and baptized. I was overjoyed, but even sometimes when we were in church I could tell Jalus did not want to get close to God. He did not want to let go of that anger. I became more concerned about Jalus getting closer to God than myself. I use to pray to God all the time for him to make Jalus happy. I didn't realize that God could not make anyone be anything. We have to want it for ourselves and allow Him to work in us.

I finally got a full time job, but Jalus was so depressed I could never be happy for myself. I would give Jalus more than half of my paycheck just to show him how much he meant to me. He would sometimes ask, "Baby, how is it that you can forgive me for abusing you so much?"

I would always smile and say, "Jalus, I love you and I want a future with you regardless of what you have done to me."

Well, a year passed and even though Jalus still said the meanest things at times, he had only hit me three times since we moved to California. It had been six months since Jalus had last hit me. Even though the physical abuse had stopped, the mental and emotional abuse continued and began making me very suicidal. Some days when Jalus would go off on me I just had to go lie down. It was like my world went crashing down all the time. I remember Lilly coming into the bedroom one day after Jalus told me the meanest things. I was just lying there crying. I could not even be a mom at times because of how bad he made me feel. Lilly said, "Mommy, did daddy make you sad again?" I cried, "Yes, Lilly, Mommy just needs to lie down for a little while." The verbal arguments were so intense at times I would be literally exhausted.

It just felt like there was always one obstacle after another with Jalus and I could never make him happy regardless of how hard I tried. I had changed so many things about myself that I didn't even know who I was any more. I changed my whole personality so Jalus would love me. It was as if I being myself meant I was beaten or yelled at for who I was. The desperation of wanting to be good enough for Jalus overtook me.

Once I had taken Jalus out for some drinks and to play pool for his birthday. We had a very nice night and he seemed like he was enjoying himself. We arrived home and I was pretty drunk and Jalus was as well. We were trying to be as quiet as possible not to wake any one up. My brother, Seth, had gone out with us too. We all ate some food and decided to head to bed. Jalus and I went into our room. I was very tired and very drunk. I had knocked out for couple minutes on the bed. I had forgotten about Jalus' rules. You see, he could fall asleep if he was too tired to have sex, but if I fell asleep first I was going to be beaten or yelled at for it.

All of a sudden I was awakened by Jalus saying, "You are so messed up you can't even give me sex on my birthday."

"Baby, I am so drunk I just fell asleep for a bit. Just let me sleep off some of the liquor." Well, that did not sit well with Jalus at all. All of a sudden, I felt a very hard slap across my face and then Jalus kicked me through our closet door.

My brother Seth busted in our room to see me on the floor in pain. Seth screamed, "You promised you would not hurt my sister again!" I ran out of the room and then, of course, my whole family was up. Everyone was yelling. It was total chaos!

Dad sat Jalus and I down again. "Jalus, why do we have to keep doing this? Do you know we all love you? Do you know my daughter loves you very much?" We talked until about 3:00 in the morning once again. I convinced my family to allow Jalus to stay, and as they always did, even though they hated what was being done to me, they let him stay. Jalus knew that in the same way I was forgiving, so was my family. Even though I knew my family was suffering from my relationship, I didn't care because I loved Jalus so much.

After about a year of this same stuff, trying my best, Jalus still wasn't happy. He still webbed everything from the past to everything I did. I could not wear certain colors anymore, not even certain hairstyles. Around this year mark, I became very suicidal. I felt like maybe if I were gone, Jalus would see how much I loved him. Maybe this pain of not being loved by someone, who I had made my whole world, would stop. I began taking up to thirty different painkillers and blood pressure pills a day. I personally believed Jalus never even noticed, and if he did, he didn't care. Jalus was all about himself and always wanting more.

Chapter Seven

"Deliver me, O Lord, from the evil man; which imagines mischiefs in his heart; Keep me, O Lord, from the hands of the wicked; preserve me from the hands of the wicked, from the hands of the violent man..."

Psalms 140:1, 2, 4

I missed Celest and Riz so bad at times. I would call them most of the time when Jalus was asleep, because I knew it was going to be an argument. Jalus would always say, "I know you talk bad about me to them."

I was absolutely depressed and stressed out. I tried to worship God as hard as I could. I finally said in prayer to God one day at work, "God, I want You to have Your will in my life." The next weekend was Mother's Day. It was nearly thirteen months since Jalus and I came to California. Jalus stated how badly he felt that he could not buy me a Mother's Day gift. I always told Jalus that all I wanted from him was to love me and treat me good. However, for some reason he didn't believe that is all I truly wanted.

Mother's Day arrived and my sister Maree and her husband, Tim, came from L. A. to celebrate with us. Jalus and

I had discussed that what he could do for me for Mother's Day was to just do something nice. But, as usual, he didn't do anything at all. It was just another day to him. I was wearing a dress and it was a pretty short one. Of course, it had upset Jalus. Evidently I had shown my underwear and Jalus became enraged after Maree and Tim left. Jalus was once again ranting and raving outside. I was in tears and my mother saw how heartbroken I was once again.

My mother finally walked outside. She heard Jalus yelling and saying things like, "You always trying show me a face and use certain colors to make me hate you." I just sat there crying feeling so hopeless and demeaned.

My mother interrupted Jalus and said, "Jalus, since you hate my daughter so much and always want to turn back into this hateful person every time we show you love, just leave."

"Good! That's exactly what I wanted to hear!" Jalus ran inside the house and began packing all of his things. I was devastated and crying hysterically. My dad approached me while Jalus was screaming through the whole house packing his things.

"Sweetheart, you have to let him go. He is never going to change. He wants that anger to stay with him and he doesn't know the meaning of grace."

Suddenly, Jalus was by the front door with his suitcase. I saw him with the $1,700 I had worked so hard for to get his green card. I became furious. "You can't take my money that I worked for!"

My brother walked up to Jalus and said, "Give me my sister's money back!"

"This is my money now and no one is taking it from me!"

My dad got in between Jalus and I. "Just let him take it so he can leave."

"How is this fair? I worked so hard for that money to make a future for us and he gets to just take it and spend it."

Jalus and I began arguing more and more until eventually my dad and brother escorted him out of the house. I stayed in the house, hearing the chaos outside. My brother and Jalus almost got into a fight. It was now midnight and that was how my Mother's Day ended. My father and brother came back inside and said he went walking up the road with his suitcase. I cried so hard. I missed him so much that I literally felt betrayed and hurt. I trusted him and believed for so long that he would change. I forgave him for so much only to find out I meant nothing to him. I was devastated. I had forgiven him every time for all of the abuse and I didn't understand how he could just throw it all away. All of the love I had dished out meant absolutely nothing to him.

I waited up all night thinking he would come back and apologize. I finally cried myself to sleep around 4:00 a.m. I awoke to see Jalus was nowhere in the house and now I had to explain to my children that daddy left. I had to be at work at 9:00 in the morning that day. I felt so empty and worried sick. Thoughts raced in my mind and I wondered if Jalus was ok. I asked my parents if they could call his mom and see if she knew where he was. They did call and I found out he was already on a plane to the island. I could not believe he left. I was barely able to manage my emotions at work. Jalus always made me believe that we would have a future. I just felt like all my hope was ripped right out of me. I felt like all of the abuse I had endured and forgave him for was for absolutely nothing. We had just got married two months earlier. I literally felt like every dream I had for us was gone. The man I tried so hard to change and show love to, gave up and decided to keep that hate imbedded in his spirit.

That night after work I arrived home and was in a totally mental state. It hurt so bad to go home and see that Jalus wasn't there. Now I know you may think I should have been happy, but him being gone left a void, a sense of failure and the feeling that I could not go on. I called Jalus' mother's phone and asked to speak to him.

"Jalus, how could you just leave the kids and I like this?"

"I am sorry, babe, I just couldn't take the living situation any more. It was not you. I am sorry."

Jalus and I talked for about three days and were getting back on good terms. I had spent $300 dollars on phone calls to call the island and talk to him.

Jalus that he was going to save some money and come back up in a couple of months after he got a job and worked for a little bit on the island. I missed him so much and couldn't even function.

On the fourth day after he left, I was taking my driving test so I could drive in the United States. I was trying to work so hard and get everything sorted out so I could get him back up. I had my father even go on a lease with me so I could get a car. The minute I was walking in to take my test I got a call from Jalus.

"So someone told me all this stuff about you when we broke up right before Israel was born. I hate you! Forget you! Forget the kids! I am never coming back!" Then he hung up.

I could not believe what had just happened. With all the grace I had given Jalus and all the pain he caused the kids and me, he still wanted to live in the past. I held no grudges against Jalus and yet he wanted to hold everything against me. I tried calling back after my test, but he turned off his phone. I was devastated and I wondered who could be so cruel to ruin our marriage. I cried everyday. I didn't eat anything for days.

Jalus then began sending me horrible texts. One of them said *I hope you and the kids die. I am going to screw all the women I want now.* When I received that text it broke my heart into a million pieces. I became suicidal and for a week Jalus and I had not spoken. I prayed to God one night to help me and help me stop hurting so much.

Then for the first time in my life I heard God speak to me. Now it's hard to explain how God spoke to me, it wasn't audible. It was a voice in my mind and my heart. I knew it was God because I had so much peace in what He said. As I was lying on my parents' couch crying because I missed Jalus so much, I heard God speak to my mind and heart. He said, "I will love you and kiss you good night and I will always be here to hold you when you cry." That night I had so much peace, a peace that I had never had before.

I awoke the next morning and I let my emotions take back over. I didn't want to trust God. I just wanted Jalus. As all of us seem to do, we choose sometimes to ignore God. I sat at work on my lunch break and let my mind take me where it should not have gone. I thought how is God going to hold me at night? I need Jalus to have that comfort. I disregarded what God had spoken to me.

Then one night Jalus and I began talking again. "I want to make the marriage to work, Babe."

Of course, like I always did, I took him back and agreed. I thought maybe we could make it work. Jalus admitted that when he left California that he went to a strip club in Los Angeles. He admitted that he had spent practically all the $1,700 I had worked for. My heart was broken when I heard this. But as I always did I showed him grace and forgave him once again. The new plan was for me to get everything set up in California so he could move back up. I started on it immediately, but the strain was too hard for my spirit. Jalus had finally got a job on the island. I felt like taking him from that job would be setting him back. He always said, "If I had a job then I would be happy." So I believed him. I thought it makes more sense to move down there so he can keep his job and his pride.

The conversations were getting so hard. I missed Jalus and he missed me. I could barely go to work and I was never happy anymore. I didn't realize how much Jalus was my world until then. I just felt so alone and the family that I so wanted with Jalus was separated and shattered into a thousand tiny pieces. Around the three-week mark since Jalus had left, I had finally reached my breaking point. I quit my job and Jalus said he was going to take care of me. For once he was going to be the provider. I believed and trusted he would take care of me. The day after I quit my job I began packing. I was waiting to receive my last paycheck.

I was getting so happy to see Jalus. Then suddenly I had a very nervous feeling come over me. It was a feeling that I couldn't shake. As I finished packing my clothes, I saw some underwear that I had that was the color Jalus always said reminded him of Dale. But Jalus told me that he didn't feel that way about anything anymore. While I was getting ready to put the underwear in my suitcase and pay the color no mind anymore, that feeling came back and then I had a vision. It was an "open" vision. Now, a vision comes from God, sometimes showing you great things and sometimes warning you from bad. The vision I saw was Jalus angrier than ever. I was curled up in a ball in excruciating pain. I saw Jalus hitting me as hard as he could with those eyes of rage. I was startled by what I saw. Jalus sounded so changed on the phone. I decided to at least call Jalus and ask him.

"Jalus when I come back to the island, do you promise you will not beat me up anymore?"

"Come on, Babe, I haven't hit you in five months. Why do you think I would go back to that?"

That was settled and I believed him, despite the warning God gave me. I decided to leave Lilly in California with my parents until I got a job on the island. Jalus said he always wanted to be the provider, so I thought this would be great. Even Jalus said he had no reason to be upset with anything. I decided to bring Israel, so off Israel and I flew to the island, even though my parents were very scared that something was going to happen.

During the whole flight Israel was very fussy. He had even knocked a hot cup of coffee right in to my lap. I was in such adrenaline mode that I didn't feel it. I just wanted to be with Jalus. I felt like being with Jalus would make me feel normal again. I so wanted just to go sleep and have him next to me. I somehow could not accept failing in the one relationship that I had given my all to. I guess trying to change for someone and change everything about you eventually makes you lose yourself.

Finally Israel and I arrived on the island, but I felt almost like God was nowhere around. I felt lost, like I truly didn't understand how I was still enduring someone who hurt me so badly. I loved Jalus so much that in some sick way it felt normal to be with him. Israel and I walked out of the airport waiting for Jalus to pick us up. At the time Jalus was living with his parents and that was going be where we would be staying. As I was standing outside the airport holding Israel, suddenly there was Jalus. He came out of his mother's car. Jalus had a smile that reached ear to ear on his face. I was overjoyed to see Jalus and so was Israel. Jalus walked up to us and swooped Israel and I in his arms. It was like being away from each other had reignited that love. Jalus put our bags in his mother's car. It was surreal being on the island again. Being in a place where everything and everyone was familiar. Jalus kept kissing me and saying, "I missed you guys, Baby."

His mother was driving and then she said, "All right you two, that's enough." I felt bad when she said this because she didn't realize that getting affection that was actually love from Jalus was rare. Most of the time affection from Jalus was based on the fact that he wanted sex.

We finally arrived at Jalus' parent's house. The first week was wonderful. I guess beside the fact that Jalus had mentioned his brother, Zalan, was the one who brought up the past, which made Jalus and I stop talking in the first place. But I didn't hold a grudge against Zalan. I knew Zalan hung around a lot of people who hated me. I showed Zalan that I had no problem with him despite the drama he had caused. It was kind of tense for the first couple of weeks, not between Jalus and me, but whenever Zalan would come by the house it became a little tense. I began to realize, however, some things about Jalus around the third week. I found out Jalus had talked to one of his ex-girlfriends on Facebook. I am not going to lie, I was angry at first, but I let it go. Then I found out Jalus had also attended a huge concert while we weren't talking. Of course, I let that go too. It was hard, though, knowing he had started living his life so quickly. I mean, while we were split up, I was devastated and didn't know how to live. It just seemed pretty sad that I made Jalus my whole world and he practically didn't even care enough to let me be even a small part of his life after all these years.

Of course, it wasn't long before that awesome love we had when we first saw each other at the airport eventually began to fade away. I would stay home and take care of Israel all day while Jalus went to work. Jalus' mother had a helper who cleaned the house and tended to his father. The helper, Alice, and I became friends. She was nice and a wise woman to talk with. When Jalus got paid, that's when I realized Jalus was just for Jalus. Now that the tables had turned, everything Jalus had said about wanting to take care of Israel and me was all a lie. Jalus got paid $600.00 and spent every dime of his money on a car. I voiced my opinion and said he was going to leave our little family broke just so he could have a car. That is when I realized him taking care of the kids and me was all a big lie. He only cared about himself. I still tried to push through.

Eventually Jalus stopped helping me with Israel. I asked him once to bathe Israel. "Taking care of kids is a woman's job."

Israel and I were not allowed to leave the house to even go for walks. We were restricted to the yard. The physical abuse had not resumed yet, so I felt like at least Jalus had changed some. That is until one day Jalus came home mad because he wasn't making enough money. He was so unpredictable! He and I could have been on the greatest terms in the morning before he left, and then when he would come home everything would turn to chaos. He would be so negative and start yelling at me. Jalus came home that day with an attitude and hated everything and everybody.

He screamed, "Get Israel dressed because my mom is too busy to watch him."

I was dressing Israel as quickly as possible. As I dressed Israel, I asked Jalus if he could buy our son a pair of shoes and some clothes. Israel had grown out of pretty much everything. My family and I were the ones who bought both my kids everything up to that point. I thought, considering Israel was his son, it wouldn't be too much to ask.

"Maybe I will after I get my car fixed."

I just frowned and continued looking for a shirt for Israel. I found a shirt that fit him and looked ok. The minute I put the shirt on Israel Jalus screamed, "Take that stupid shirt off him!"

"Why, Babe, it has no holes and it actually fits him."

Jalus walked up and jerked the shirt off Israel. I just looked at Jalus, confused.

"You always have to show me a face, huh?"

"What are you talking about? I dressed Israel just like you asked."

Then suddenly Jalus walked up and slapped me very hard across my face.

I was shocked, "What the hell did I do wrong?" I asked, crying.

Israel was just watching in fear of what his father had just done. Israel was fully aware now when mommy was hurt.

Jalus screamed, "You know I hate that fucking color, you spiteful bitch!"

"Jalus, you promised that you would stop living in the past. How is this fair when I don't ever relate anything of the past with you?" Jalus walked off and "kissed his teeth." That is the sound and gesture that means, "Kiss my ass!"

Jalus later apologized and stated that he felt I was always doing everything to bring up the past. Even though Jalus apologized I knew that this was just the beginning again of the physical abuse. If Jalus slapped me once, a harder beating was coming. I never knew when, but I knew for certain it was coming. My self-esteem was shattered once again. I felt maybe if I was more beautiful and skinnier Jalus would love me more. I gave Jalus full forgiveness, yet again, and told him he was my world.

My parents would call and ask how I was doing. I would lie and tell them Jalus was treating me good. I wanted this to be true so badly. I would talk to Lilly and I could tell she missed me as much as I missed her.

Jalus had totally forgotten about God. On the island showing compassion and love for God was a sign of weakness. He had totally forgotten about how God let him feel His Holy Spirit. I could barely feel God's presence anymore either. God felt so far away. I would lift my hands up and try to feel God's Holy Spirit and felt nothing. The Holy Spirit is God's presence. I know it sounds a little crazy, but when you actually feel God's Holy Spirit, you know He is real. It's an actual sensation in your body that makes you feel higher than any drug could possibly make you and you have more peace than you have ever had in your entire life. It's like God is literally holding you in His arms.

Jalus just wanted more money now. Jalus would make so many plans and yet none of them involved God. Jalus was unhappy. He had a job, money, a car and was still not happy. He kept promising me that if he had more money then he would be happy and treat me well. I watched Christian shows and prayed all the time, asking God to fix Jalus and our marriage. The only time Jalus spent money on me or Israel was for food or cigarettes. Honestly I was fine with this. I never wanted Jalus to spend money on me. I just wanted him to love me and treat me right. That's all I wanted. But for some reason it was impossible for Jalus to do.

Then the night came when Jalus started an argument. He had a bad day at work. As usual, it lead to the past and Jalus relating every facial expression I made and everything I wore to the past. I was tired of being yelled at and constantly walking on eggshells and living in the world of Jalus where almost anything and everything I did was offensive to him. Jalus continued arguing with me until midnight. I was so exhausted. I even tried to defuse the argument and kept telling him, "Baby, let's not argue over stuff from the past and just go to sleep." But Jalus was always in control. The arguments that he started would not end until he decided they would end. I finally just walked into our room and decided to lie down on the bed. Israel was asleep on the bed that we made him on the ground. Jalus came into the room moments afterward still yelling.

"Jalus, Israel is sleeping and I am tired. I don't want Israel to wake up—we both know I am going to have to put him back to sleep."

"You're so stupid! You always showing me a face."

"Jalus, I am sorry for whatever I have done wrong. Let's just go to sleep, please."

Finally, Jalus lay down in our bed next to me. I was lying on my stomach and something in me just felt uneasy. "You're such a spiteful bitch."

"No, I am not."

Within a second of me saying that, Jalus struck me with his fist in my head. I grabbed my head in pain and began to cry. I just rolled over to the edge of the bed curled up in pain. Then I had the scariest vision of my life. It was an open vision again. I saw Jalus on top of me beating me as hard as he could. I heard my screams of pain and it was worst beating I have ever received in my life. After I saw this, fear took over and my heart began to race. Then just like I had seen in the vision, "You going to keep being spiteful?" Before I could even reply Jalus jumped on top of my chest and pinned me down. Fist after fist each punch got harder and harder. I screamed in pain and fear, but the punches kept coming. I was trying to protect my face but Jalus held my hands so he could punch my face and head as hard and he could. I felt dizzy and the pain was so intense. I knew Jalus had lost complete control. He was hitting me like he was hitting a man his size. I tried kicking him off, Jalus caught my legs with his arms and for one second it looked like he was shocked at what he was doing. It was as if he had actually come back to his senses and realized the monster he had become. However, he ignored it and rage once again took over. Jalus continued the beating. By this point I was screaming at the top of my lungs in fear and pain. Begging Jalus to stop. Suddenly, Israel awoke screaming. Jalus stopped the beating and turned on the lights while standing on the bed over my beaten body. Jalus paid Israel no mind and then Jalus began kicking me in my face and head stomping on me while he was standing on the bed.

"Jalus, please stop, for the sake of Israel at least!" Jalus then jumped off the bed.

"Please stop? Watch this!" Jalus grabbed a hard plastic clothes hamper filled with clothes. The container was probably about fifty pounds. He then jumped back on the bed and before I could manage to get up and off the bed, he held the container and hit me with it five times. I felt weak and knew I was badly hurt. I was praying to God in my mind to save me. Finally, Jalus stopped. Israel was still screaming at seeing me being beaten by his father. I pushed every last bit of energy I had to get off the bed. I knew I had to get out of the room. I knew my life depended on it.

I ran towards Israel and said, "Mommy is ok, Baby." Deep down I knew I was not ok. I felt my face like it was on fire and my head started swelling. My whole body felt like it was shutting down. Jalus was on the other side of the room pacing up and down. That rage was still within him. I knew I couldn't take any more hits.

"I'm going to get Israel a bottle," I said, running out the door of our bedroom. I knew I had to get out of that room before Jalus could even respond. Israel and I were in the kitchen. I saw Jalus pacing up and down in the room. I was watching for Jalus. I hoped he wouldn't beat me out in the kitchen. His mom and dad would hear. I was watching the bottle in the microwave. My body was in complete agony. I didn't know what was wrong, but I knew the condition of my body was bad. Then the bottle was done.

Suddenly, Jalus ran up to me, "You need to leave or I'm going to kill you! Leave now!" he screamed. I just stood there in fear. Just like all the other fights either way I wasn't going to say the right thing. Either way I was going to get beaten.

Then saw I saw his mother's door opening. I thought I wouldn't be beaten anymore. But then Jalus looked at his mother while she was walking out of her room and he grabbed me by my hair and delivered four more punches to my head and face. I partially blacked out for a few seconds and felt dizzy and very weak. I heard his mother screaming at him. She pulled him off of me and led me to her room.

His mother then said to me, "This is no life and this is not love." His mother told me to lie down in her bed with her. I was in severe pain, but I was so tired. I awoke four hours later.

I was in the most pain I have ever experienced in my entire life. I could barely see out of my right eye and my whole body ached. I had swelling all over my head and my face felt numb from being so swollen. I remember hearing Jalus trying to convince his mother to let him talk to me. She was being very persistent. Then I decided to walk out of her room.

The minute I walked out, both of their jaws dropped.

Chapter Eight

"You've got to be willing to lose everything to gain yourself."
—Iyanla Vanzant

Jalus had done such a number on me this time it even shocked him. My nerves were on edge when I walked out and saw their reactions. I still had not got up the courage to look at my face. But from the reaction I got, and how badly my body felt, I figured it was really bad. Jalus' mom gasped at the damage that her Jalus had done.

Jalus softened his voice, "Baby, please come talk to me in the bathroom." He guided me to the bathroom, holding my hand. When we walked into the bathroom I saw my face in the mirror. The damage was shocking. I had bruises and swelling from my head straight down. The entire right side of my face was swollen and my eye was swollen shut. I just broke down crying in disbelief.

"Baby, I will understand if you want to leave me." I was still in shock and I had nowhere to go even if I wanted to leave. "I am so sorry and I will take you to the hospital once I get off work."

"Yeah, ok, Jalus."

I'm not going lie. I was just so deathly afraid of Jalus now. I didn't even know how to react to it all. I had to take care of Israel and I was in so much pain. I wore sunglasses all that day. Alice was cleaning the house and I decided to watch a Christian program. I was just feeling so lost and in pain. Suddenly, I saw a man on the television saying we were meant to guard our heart for God only. That was a new concept to me. My whole life I wore my heart on my sleeve, especially with Jalus. For some reason, those words seemed so right. I started saying it and I would touch my heart. "God, please guard my heart."

Jalus finally arrived home from work. I was in extreme pain by the time he arrived. I was in so much pain I honestly didn't care how scared I was of him. When he walked through the door I said, "What the hell took you so long?" I was in tears considering how much pain I was in.

"I had stuff to do."

I got ready to go to the hospital.

Jalus' mom stopped us from going out of the house. "Where are you guys going?"

"I am taking her to the hospital."

"You know they will arrest you, Jalus."

"I am going to say I fell down a flight of stairs." So off we went to see what damage was to my body. Jalus and Israel stayed in the car while I walked into the hospital.

The hospital checked me in and did x-rays. They had me on an IV for pain. I just sat there not knowing what was wrong. My mind raced with the fact that this was my life. The life of lying and covering for Jalus and about two hours went by.

Then the doctor walked in. "We need to keep you overnight due to your injuries."

I knew I must have been in bad shape. I knew I needed to stay in the hospital, but I knew Jalus wouldn't agree.

"Honestly, Doctor, I can't stay overnight." The doctor explained that I needed a CT scan and needed to be monitored. I eventually gave up on convincing the doctor to let me leave. So I asked, "May I use the bathroom?" I went towards the bathroom with the IV needle still in my hand.

I then bolted towards the exit and ran to the car where Jalus and Israel were. As I got in the car Jalus was totally frustrated. "What took you so long?" he asked.

"I'm really hurt and they wanted to keep me overnight."

Jalus totally disregarded it and said he would stop by the pharmacy to get me some cheap painkillers. Because I left, they didn't give me any painkillers. I was stuck in extreme pain. While we were driving home I started to try to remove the IV needle from my hand. Because I had never removed an IV before, the minute I got it out, blood came gushing out.

"Don't get blood on the car!" About 10 minutes before we got home he asked, "Why do you always do stuff to get me so mad?"

As usual, I was the one to blame in Jalus' mind. I thought how could I make Jalus stop. So I did the craziest thing, considering Jalus was a "schizo." I replied, "I am schizophrenic, Jalus."

Now I know that sounds absolutely crazy, but I thought maybe if I pretended that, he wouldn't hit me anymore and stop relating everything. I mean, I would even be beaten for wearing certain colors. I just needed something to buy me some time. I was so in love with Jalus and didn't understand why he went back to this crazy Jalus all the time. I loved him, but I was deathly afraid of him now. I was hooked. I figured if he ends up killing me at least he would see I never gave up on him. I continued to say, "God, please guard my heart and mind." I said that everyday of that week and then the weekend came. Jalus had promised the week before that he would get me out of the house.

However, now that I had bruises all over me Jalus said we couldn't go out. As usual, Jalus said I was making him look bad and people would talk. Whenever I saw anyone that week, I told them I had fallen down the stairs. I covered for Jalus once again and cared more about his feelings than mine. I noticed that urge I used to have to impress Jalus and make him love me was starting to fade. Every time I said, "God, please guard my heart and mind," I felt I was disconnecting from Jalus.

I convinced Jalus to take me out. I just needed to get out of that house. We had only been out two times before this and Jalus argued with me the next day. Jalus told me to cover up my bruises. I piled on the makeup to cover my black eye and the bruises. I had become very skilled on covering up my bruises and making up great stories to explain why I had the ones I couldn't cover up. I had made up such a great story that most of the people we knew had already heard the story. I was very convincing and Jalus always went along with it.

Jalus decided that our night out was going to be at the bar by his house. The minute we arrived, Jalus was already not talking and being very antisocial. I never understood it. Jalus had ordered us both a drink. Then his baby cousin, Shelly, came by us to say hi. The minute Shelly walked up her facial expression changed. She asked, "What happened to you? Why you all bruised up?" She gave me that look that every girl that has been abused gives. That look that says *I am sorry you're going through this.*

Of course, I covered by saying, "Oh, girl, I got so high I fell off a chair and down some stairs." Even though I was telling this funny story, I knew that deep down this smile and laugh was hiding a truly painful lie. I have known Shelly for years. She was a very gorgeous girl. She was probably a couple years younger than me. She was always a great friend.

The night went on and out of nowhere my cousin Jamie appeared. She normally wasn't on my side of the district. But for some reason tonight she was. She walked up and said hi and gave me a hug. My cousin, Jaime, has never been stupid. The minute she saw the bruises she shouted, "What the hell? Did Jalus do that to you?" I denied it. I told her the same story I was telling everyone. Jalus was hanging out with his friends while I was socializing with Jaime.

"If he did that to you I want to know because I will kick his ass. You're my cousin."

I laughed, "Na he didn't." I wished I could say yes, but I was living with him and I truly didn't know what to do. I went into the bar to get another drink. Walking out I saw one of my good friends that I used to hang out with when I was dating Cray. Zelle was an awesome girl and tough as hell. Back in the day, Zelle and her big sister, Mimi, always had my back. All of the other girls in our group back then were always there for me, as well. I had and still have tons of respect for those girls. I gave Zelle this biggest hug ever. It was like we hadn't seen each other in years, which we really hadn't.

Zelle said, "Mimi and I were just talking about you the other day and how you were always so nice and funny." When she said this it made me feel so good that I was actually loved for who I was. Jalus had made me feel that I was so annoying and a person who needed to change every part of me.

Zelle, Jaime and I talked a lot. Jalus wasn't talking. I was so drunk by this time and I hadn't felt this much love and appreciation in such a long time. It felt good knowing I was great just the way I was. I honestly didn't realize exactly how much pain I was in until that moment. I was almost immune to be beaten. I had bruises all over me and I just kept denying how dark my life actually was. The "me" that was always happy and positive wasn't there anymore. It was all a cover up now.

Jalus and I went home that night, and thank God we didn't argue. Something in me just knew my body couldn't take another beating. I continued to pretend like I was a "schizo." I guess you could call it "an act of survival."

The next morning Jalus and I started off the morning ok. Jalus was in a decent mood. However, I was experiencing something very strange. I had been saying, "God, guard my heart and mind," for almost six days now. I felt that morning like I missed the "old me." Even though I fought my pain by numbing it with alcohol and weed, I still knew me. I began thinking that I was about to turn twenty-three. Was this truly going to be my life? Was I really ready to live the life of an abused wife and mother? I didn't want to be the woman who had so many dreams and never fulfilled one because she was forced to change everything about her. The man that she ran to and made her feel on top of the world was now the man who crushed everything in her world.

Jalus spoke and broke my chain of thoughts. "Do you even love me anymore?"

I just looked at him. For once, something in me knew I wasn't in love with him anymore, as though the control he had on me was gone. The woman who lived every second to make him happy was finally breaking free. I cared more about what God thought of me. I cared more now about what people who loved me and cherished me thought.

"I love you, but something just feels different."

Right after I said that, I decided to go inside and get something to drink. Israel was inside with Jalus' mother. Zalan was in their mother's room. Israel had run in their room so I went in to get him. I had been hiding my bruises pretty much all week. Since I was at the house and it wasn't even noon yet, I wasn't covering any. I wasn't expecting any one to be see me.

As I walked into the room I saw Zalan. I didn't make much eye contact because honestly I knew from the look on his face he was shocked at how bruised I was. I felt his eyes observing all the bruises. You see, I literally was bruised from head to toe. I got Israel and walked out. I went back outside to find Jalus rolling up some weed.

Suddenly, I got a call from a strange number. To my surprise it was Celest. She said, "Hey, Girl, I'm on the island. Where are you?"

"I'm at Jalus'."

"I'm coming to see you right now. Be there in a sec."

Now I was very happy to know Celest was coming to see me. Then the minute I got off the phone with her I looked down at my legs. I remembered I was bruised from head to toe. I questioned, would I be able to convince Celest that this was a goofy mistake? Or would she realize her best friend was beaten worse than she had ever seen me?

I looked up and Jalus asked, "Celest is coming here? What the hell you going tell her about why you are all bruised up?"

By the time those words came out of his mouth, Celest pulled up. As I walked towards her I started to pretend to laugh. I said, "Oh, Girl, you see what happens to me when I get high and fll off a chair down some stairs?" Celest laughed along with me, but she gave me that look like she knew the truth.

Celest didn't stay long, but we did get caught up with each other. Honestly, I couldn't talk much in front of Jalus. He would take everything and twist it so he could be offended. The weekend was now almost over. Seven days since the beating. I was still in a lot of pain and tried to stay high and on pills to control it. I honestly did wonder what was wrong with my body and why it was taking so long to heal.

It was Monday and Jalus had gone to work. Something about me felt very strange, as though I wasn't trying to please Jalus anymore. I was actually more concerned about how to please God. I noticed how sad Israel looked. I knew how bad he just wanted to go on a walk and get out the house. Suddenly, I decided I was going to take my son to the water. There was a beach about a five-minute walk from us. I put on Israel's shoes. He already had a smile from ear to ear. I was worried, but I figured Jalus wouldn't be home for a couple of hours. So off Israel and I went to go look at the ocean. The craziest thing happened while we were walking. The farther I got from the house, the freer I felt.

How good it felt to be able to walk out of the house when I pleased. It felt good not having to ask permission to enjoy life and the beauty of nature. Israel and I finally reached the beach and Israel could not stop smiling. As I looked out on the ocean I heard God actually speak to my heart. He said, "There is so much more to life than the one you are living." For some strange reason, this felt so right to me. It felt so good to be able to be spontaneous and enjoy life, how much I truly just wanted to enjoy life and to see my son so happy.

I looked at my phone and realized Jalus would soon be arriving home. Israel and I walked back to the house. About fifteen minutes later Jalus walked through the door. I greeted him with a smile and a kiss. Last time I checked we where suppose to be all right. However, Jalus had that angry face again. I knew that from that looks of things, there was going to be a beating tonight. Always hoping I could defuse the anger I asked, "Jalus, what's wrong?" He just gave me that silent treatment.

I was honestly frustrated that Jalus was miserable once again. He had a job, a car and money. He also had just gone to an interview. So I responded to Jalus, "Why can't you just smile and be happy?"

"Smile? You always trying to show me a face and be on those pussies' side."

I was very confused. "Jalus, what the hell are you talking about now?"

"You know you relating to Ty when you say that cause you're happy my tooth got knocked out." Jalus screamed.

Tears started running down my cheeks. "Jalus, that has nothing to do with me telling you to smile and be happy." Jalus just walked in the house mad as ever.

His mother came up and asked, "What's wrong with Jalus now?"

I explained calmly to Jalus' mother evidently what I did wrong.

His mother said, "He is mad because I said something about his smile earlier so he is taking it out on you. He is just being ridiculous."

I was very concerned about this argument. My body was still very weak and sore from the last beating I received. I knew if this didn't defuse quickly I was going to be beaten again tonight. I tried talking to Jalus about it and telling him it made no sense relating everything to past situations.

I saw Jalus ranting and raving. I was in tears and I went in the bathroom like I always did over this last week. I looked in the mirror and said, "God, guard my heart and mind." I walked out feeling empowered, and for once since I met Jalus, I was ready to leave him for good. Something in me felt like if I stayed for this beating it was going to be my last. I knew I had to leave, and this time there was no coming back. I had numbed the pain in my body for a week by taking pills and smoking weed every hour. I just knew if I was going to be beaten again this soon, that my body would totally give out.

It was either, I leave and live life without Jalus or I stay and play Russian Roulette with my life. I knew if I was going to leave that night, then I was going to need someone to come get me and help me until I figured out a plan. It was around 5:00 in the evening and Jalus was ranting and saying horrible things about me. Somehow I was responsible for what his mother had done.

I saw the rage building in his eyes. By now I knew I had about an hour and a half before the beating would start. His mother walked out and left the house. I knew what would happen if I stayed. I walked off from Jalus, even though he was still yelling and I called Celest.

"Celest, I need you to come get me or Jalus is going to beat me up bad tonight."

Celest heard the fear in my voice. "I will be there soon, Babe."

Jalus eventually gave me a very pathetic apology. "I'm sorry for what I said, but it's you who makes things like this happen."

The fact of the matter was that after almost four years of being together he was still doing this. Jalus had reverted back to the Jalus that made me fear for my life.

Deep down, even though I had overlooked it all these years, I knew there was no changing him. He didn't want to change and didn't think he needed to change anything about himself. When Jalus saw that I had actually begun packing my bags he started ranting again. I knew Celest would be there in about fifteen minutes now. I had to avoid being in the room with Jalus. Israel was walking around and I could tell he was confused. I knew I was going to have to leave Israel with Jalus. I knew I wasn't going to have any money or food. I was going to have to jump houses and figure out how to get Israel. I didn't even have a plan, yet I just knew God mattered more to me then Jalus and I couldn't keep living like this. Jalus screamed, "You will miss me!"

"I will have God with me," I replied.

"Yeah, I will have Him with me too!" he screamed. I knew things were going to get bad in a very short time. I began praying to God that Celest would show up quickly. I was honestly scared. I knew my body was severely injured. I had no idea what was wrong, but I knew it wasn't good. I could see Jalus beginning to pace up and down again saying horrible things to me. Suddenly, I saw headlights driving up. It was Celest. The minute I saw her I ran towards her.

She asked, "Are you ok, Hun?"

"Yea, I'm alright. I need you to get my bags, though, they are in the room." I looked at the front door of the house and saw Jalus appear. Celest and I walked toward the door to get my bags. Jalus said, "So you're leaving?"

"Yes, Jalus, I am leaving."

"You're not taking Israel with you, I hope you know."

I already knew that I wasn't going to anyway. I had no way to take care of him. "Fine, Jalus, you can keep him for now." Celest was standing between us. Jalus got that look in his eyes. That rage that didn't care who was there.

"Fuck you, Bitch!" Jalus screamed and then threw the orange juice that he was drinking on me.

Celest screamed, "Jalus, what the hell?"

Celest told me to get in the car. I started walking towards it. Jalus followed behind us screaming. I jumped in and Celest locked the door behind me.

Celest remained outside the car. Jalus was screaming at her. Then somehow Celest convinced him to let her get my bags. I saw Celest and Jalus walking into the house. I was upset at myself that my best friend had to do this for me. I was upset for putting her in the middle of this. I just sat there praying Jalus wouldn't do anything to her. I thought about this and realized how afraid I was of my own husband.

I had overheard in the screaming from earlier when Celest had locked me in the car that Jalus had switched up his argument and evidently wanted me to take Israel now. Celest also knew I wasn't going to be able to take care of him because I didn't have any where to live now. I then saw Celest with my bags and she walked to the car. Jalus was still out of sight. Then right when Celest reached the car Jalus appeared out of the front door with Israel at his side. I can't lie when I saw Israel standing with Jalus I wanted to take him with me. I love my children so much and hated to be without them. But I knew I had no way to provide for Israel and no place for him to stay. I also knew that if I stayed my children would keep seeing their mother being beaten. I prayed to God that he would protect Israel. I knew I would get my son back, but not knowing when was killing me.

Celest then broke my chain of thought.

"I told Jalus we would take Israel, but I was just going along with it so he would let me take your bags."

I responded, "Yeah, Doll, you know how it is. I don't even have money to provide for my son. Jalus is just thinking about himself. He doesn't care that I have no money and no way to feed my son."

Celest drove off and I looked at Jalus with his hands up. Of course, he was probably pissed off because we had not obeyed his commands that I take Israel. We headed to Celest's house and as we were about to turn onto her road I saw headlights by her house and they where blue headlights just like the ones Jalus had on his car.

I screamed, "Celest, that's Jalus! Turn around!"

"What the hell is he doing by my house?" Celest responded. She turned the car around immediately and we drove to a nearby dock. Celest and I talked for about ten minutes. Celest decided it should be safe to go back to her house. As we drove up I saw there was no car there so I was relieved. Yet I had major anxiety that Jalus was around and going to hurt me. As Celest walked me into her house I stayed very close to her. I feared that Jalus was going to jump out from somewhere and attack me. As Celest and I walked into her house, we saw her mom, Mrs. Zoe.

Mrs. Zoe was a very friendly, beautiful woman. She has known me from the time Celest and I had become best friends, around ten years ago. Mrs. Zoe greeted me with that warm, friendly smile of hers. I asked to use their phone to let my parents know what was happening. I explained to my parents what happened and they said it would take some time for them to try to get some money together to get me back to the States.

Celest asked if I wanted to smoke some weed with her. Of course, I didn't decline the offer. Celest and I began walking over to her neighbor's house. I was still covered in the orange juice that Jalus had thrown on me. As Celest and I approached her neighbor's house I was looking all over to make sure Jalus wasn't around. I realized how messed up it was to have to be so scared and paranoid. To think the person I feared so greatly was my own husband! As Celest went to introduce us I realized I knew the guy. It was Kent, a guy I knew from when I was younger. Kent and I had never had conversations, though, we just knew each other casually.

Most of the time I got him confused with his twin brother, Trent. I greeted Kent and we began to get high. For once in my life, I decided to tell a little about what I was going through. I talked to Kent and Celest about the abuse with Jalus. Of course, I didn't go into explicit details. When Kent heard my story he said, "That's messed up. I have never put my paws on a female." It was nice hearing the opinion of a real man and realizing that what I was going through wasn't a normal way of life. Celest asked if I was ready go back to her house and get some sleep. I agreed immediately. I was exhausted emotionally, mentally and physically. When we got back to Celest's house, we talked a bit about the situation and what I was going to do. Celest suggested I get Israel and head back to California as quickly as possible.

I went to sleep that night and I got the most peaceful night's sleep I could ever remember having. The next morning I awoke Celest and got ready. Before we left Celest's apartment I said a little prayer to God. I said "God, guard my heart and mind and show me the truth of the things I do not know." As we began driving, I knew Celest had to go to work and I had to find another place to be. We stopped by Riz's house to see if she was home.

Her mother, Mrs. Dia, said, "Riz is at work right now, but she should be home later."

"Ok, let her know I stopped by." I walked back to the car. I told Celest to take me by my aunt's house. Going to my aunt's was truly my last resort. Now it's not that my father's family didn't like me, it's just I had distanced myself from them. I probably had not even shown up to a family event from the time I was fifteen. I felt bad having to ask my dad's family for anything, especially for food, a place to sleep and safety. But I had go somewhere during the day while Celest was at work.

Celest understood that I was not that close with my dad's family, but she also knew I needed support from her and Riz so that I would not be tempted to go back to Jalus. Celest dropped me off at my aunt's house. "Celest, make sure you come get me when as soon as you are done with work, please."

"Oh, girl, you know I will. Just you be safe."

I walked into my uncle's house. He was my dad's older brother. They all greeted me with smiles and love like they always did. Honestly, I knew my dad's family would never desert me. It's just their house was already full of people and I have never been so low in my life that I literally had nowhere to go and no idea how I was going to get by. I felt extremely bad because Celest was going through a very hard time as well. One of her very close guy friends had just died in a motorcycle accident. I knew it affected Celest and I just felt like a burden to everyone.

I was the best friend that normally had it all together; money, a car, a job and my own place, but now I was the one leaning on my best friends for nearly everything just to survive. I sat there at my uncle's house in deep thought on how my life was falling so horribly apart. My body was still bruised and achy, but I seemed to numb every bit of pain I was feeling. I texted Riz and told her I wanted to come see her. She texted me when she got off work.

At the same time Riz got off work Celest came and picked me up. We both headed to Riz's house. I had to keep praying, "God, guard my heart and mind." For some strange reason I kept missing Jalus. But every time I said, "God, guard my heart and mind," the emptiness of missing Jalus stopped and I was reminded of the pain that he caused me.

When we arrived at Riz's house I saw Riz's brother Ray and his son. I was honestly shocked at how much time had passed. I remember Ray's son when he was very young. Now he was almost a teenager. Riz greeted Celest and I. I was overjoyed to see Riz and I gave her a hug, "How you been, Girl?" Riz smiled and we all began talking. Some of Riz's other friends were there also.

Chapter Nine

"God will not be absent when his people are on trial; He will stand in as their advocate, to plead on their behalf."

–Charles Spurgeon

While we talked that evening, Riz shared something I was unaware of. Liza had told her that when Jalus had came back to the island he called her and tried to get together with her. When I heard that I began laughing hysterically. Celest and Riz asked, "Are you ok, Ma?"

"Oh, yeah, I'm great." I thought it was funny as hell that Jalus had made himself sound so perfect when in reality he had taken my money and left our children. The minute he landed on the island had decided to talk to Liza and covered it up this whole time. I just sat there smoking weed with Riz and Celest thinking my husband beats me and cheats on me. Why could I possibly ever want him back? God had now revealed another reason why I needed to leave for good.

"Liza can have him if she wants him. I will pray that he doesn't kill her like he almost did me. I am sure that if I stayed even an hour longer, I would be dead."

Riz lightened up the conversation by saying, "Don't worry, Ma, we're going to keep you numb through this all." I laughed and took another puff on the blunt. The girls then shared how they had seen Jalus change nearly everything about me. They said they could see every time Jalus and I were around them I was on edge and scared. They said they could tell I had to watch everything I said and did around Jalus and they knew that they had to play along for my sake. I was honestly shocked that Riz and Celest saw the truth when I thought I covered it up so well. By the end of the day, I fully understood why these two women where my best friends.

I felt so lucky to have best friends like them. To have these amazing women accept me just as I was and cared for me just as much as I cared and loved them was overwhelming. I began to realize everything about me now was different. I barely smiled anymore, let alone laughed. It was like Jalus had totally changed my personality.

This was now my second night of not speaking to or seeing Jalus. Riz was going on a date with her significant other so that left me with Celest for the night. Celest and I got ready at her place and we went out. Even though I was honestly exhausted, I tagged along. Riz and Celest both knew leaving me alone for long periods of time wasn't smart. They kept me with them wherever they went. Celest and I went out and had a great night. I got absolutely drunk due to my emotions running wild. I awoke the next morning and realized I had drunkenly texted Jalus. But this text was not a nice text. I confronted Jalus saying I had found out about him talking to Liza and I said that he was officially dust to me, and that there was no way in hell we were ever getting back together.

Later that morning Jalus sent me a text saying how sorry he was and how much he and Israel missed me.

Honestly, as a mother, I wanted both of my children back in my arms. I knew, though, if I was going to get Israel it would have to be discreet and I was going to have to devise a very intelligent plan.

All that day Jalus kept texting me. I ignored him and kept saying, "God, guard my heart and mind."

Celest and Riz had evidently made a plan that I would stay with Celest for a couple nights and then stay with Riz. It was very hard, though, for me to put this kind of pressure on my friends. Riz was going through a lot. Her father had just gotten over cancer and Celest was dealing with her friend's death. I attended her friend's funeral with Celest. I was sitting in the funeral just looking at all the people crying over this young man. I tried my best to comfort my dear friend, Celest.

Suddenly, I heard God speak to my mind. "You see how this young man is known well for talking about me and living for me? If you stay with Jalus you will end up here in Heaven." When God spoke this to me my heart began racing. "People will only know you for trying your best to please Jalus and he will kill you. Once you are dead you will have to come to Heaven and face Me. I will ask you, 'What about me?'" I was in shock at what God had spoken to me during this funeral. I knew I did not want to face God and tell Him that staying with Jalus was more important to me than He was.

After the funeral I ended up going to Riz's. Celest needed time to herself. Of course I understood. I was jumping houses between Celest or Riz. They took me everywhere they went and paid for everything. Honestly, I used to be the one that treated them. That was the kind of friend I used to be. Basically, I loved being able to pay for everything and treat my friends. Knowing that they were happy was a joy and if I could help them have a great night I was happy to do it.

That night Riz took me to a house party. She paid for me to get in and we had a nice night. But while I was at this house party I saw Jalus's big brother, Zalan's ex-girlfriend who was also the mother of Zalan's daughter. Now Zalan's girlfriend and I had never really spoken much. I knew though that she had a restraining order against Zalan. When she and I saw each other I said, "Hi."

She said, "I see you are finally free."

I laughed because I knew probably most of the stuff I went through with Jalus she had probably gone through with Zalan. Riz and her girlfriend were ready to go home. We left and went to Riz's girlfriend's house.

They showed me to my room and I went right to sleep. I loved being able to talk to Riz. She always knew how to make me laugh, even through the hardest of times. At one point Riz made me laugh so hard I was crying. I thought how nice it was to laugh because of something funny instead of laughing to keep from crying because of how bad things were.

Around mid-afternoon Riz received a call from her parents and she looked shocked and upset. "Riz, what's wrong?" I asked concerned.

"Jalus just showed up at my parents' house looking for you."

I felt my heart stop for a second, and that fear that I had been trying to numb, suddenly returned.

Then Riz's phone rang and I just knew in an instinct it was Jalus when I saw the look on her face. Riz was very stern with Jalus and told him he is never to show up at her parents' house again. Evidently Jalus understood now that my phone had been off overnight and I was trying to avoid any and all contact with him. A brief second after Jalus got off the phone with Riz he began calling her phone over and over again. He wanted to speak to me. So I decided to go let Jalus have the intensity of my full temper. Everything I had been holding back and everything I now knew and felt was unleashed on him. I held absolutely nothing back!

When I heard Jalus' voice on the other end of the phone I had a feeling of disgust and absolutely no passion or love for him. Jalus was crying and telling me how much he missed me. I no longer missed him. I honestly chuckled to hear him cry. I had never heard him cry over me before. Everything about Jalus that I use to believe was such a lie. God had revealed to me how horrible Jalus truly was.

"Enjoy your time with Israel now because I am taking him with me. You will never see us again, just like you always wanted." It felt so good to say that. After I hung up the phone I became so frustrated with the fact that I had wasted almost four years of my life with Jalus and my body was still so messed up. Within two hours Jalus switched to texting. He sent a text saying that if I was not going to be with him then I would never see Israel again. I quietly prayed, "God, guard my heart and mind and please take control."

I felt such an overwhelming peace. No longer did I feel like Jalus was stronger than God. I got a call that evening from my mom saying that she got me a ticket to leave the island and I had a day to get everything done. The first thing was to find a way to get off without a passport. The second was to get Israel and avoid getting caught by Jalus. So the race was on. I called my aunt and she picked me up.

We headed to the passport office. At first the lady at the passport office said a passport would take four to six weeks to get a new one.

I knew this was not going to work. Suddenly, I prayed, "God, give me wisdom." Then wisdom came.

I said, "Well, actually I am a U.S citizen and I lost my passport."

She smiled and said, "Well, in that case, the police station can write you a letter so you can clear border control and you can travel without one." I smiled from ear to ear. God was speaking keys of wisdom to me in order to get me off the island.

I went to get Israel's birth certificate. I waited for about ten minutes. My mind was worried in turmoil afraid that Jalus would find me and figure out what I was doing. When the lady working at the office handed me Israel's birth certificate I noticed something. I smiled as I was walking out. Due to the circumstances at Israel's birth when Jalus and I had left the island a year ago when I filled out the original birth certificate, I was not able to put Jalus' name on it. Jalus never want to leave the house at that time. I had totally forgotten about that until now. I walked back to my aunt's car smiling. Knowing the fact that Jalus officially had no power, I knew God was on my side.

So everything was in order to leave, except to get Israel and avoid Jalus catching me. I went that night and slept at Riz's house. I could tell my body was worn down and so could Riz. Riz said, "Ma, I know you don't want to be left alone, but I really think you need some rest."

"Yeah, Riz, you're right." I lay there in Riz's bed and turned on a Christian program. I knew something was wrong with my body and the lump on my face. I could hardly breathe out of my nose now. Clear fluid kept running from it. For once, I fell into such a deep sleep that it was like God had told me to rest.

The next morning when I awoke, I was going to be on a plane for the States within six hours. I called my aunt, "I need us to leave now to get Israel. I have no idea when Jalus will get off work so we have to go now." Within the hour my aunt arrived, as we drove to Jalus' house my heart raced. I knew that if he caught me taking Israel it would get ugly and I would receive another beating. It would not matter who would be there to help me.

We arrived and I approached the house with caution, and then knocked. Suddenly, I saw Mrs. Alice.

She greeted me with a smile. She said, "Hello, how have you been?"

"Ok, Mrs. Alice. I have come to take Israel." She let us in the house. I walked in and saw my precious Israel. He ran up and hugged me. I held him tightly. Feeling the touch of one of my children again was like heaven on earth.

My aunt whispered, "We need to hurry." I ran into my old room. That room was filled with terrible memories of beatings and pain. I did my best to ignore them. I grabbed all of Israel's things.

Mrs. Alice said "Are you taking Israel for good?"

"Yes, Mrs. Alice, I am. Jalus beats me and I need Israel to be raised in a safe environment."

"They told me if you came to get Israel not to allow you to take him, but who am I to tell his mother she cannot take her son, especially after all you have been through?"

"Thank you, Mrs. Alice!" I picked up Israel and carried him to my aunt's car and off we went.

Israel, my aunt and I all arrived at her house and my uncle and his son greeted us. We were inside the house grabbing the rest of my things. My flight was leaving in an hour. I knew we had to move quickly. I knew that sooner or later Mrs. Alice would have to tell Jalus that I had taken Israel. I walked out into the living room and just when I was about to step outside, I heard a knock. My heart began to race and through the window I saw Jalus's eyes beaming at me.

"Open the door!" Jalus screamed. My uncle and his son walked outside to talked to Jalus.

I heard a lot of talking. For some reason I felt God was testing me to see if I could truly walk away from Jalus forever. Before I built up the courage to walk outside I prayed, "God, guard my heart and mind."

As I opened the front door and approached them, Jalus screamed, "You are not taking my son nowhere!"

I was going to play stupid. "I am not going anywhere, Jalus, what are you talking about?"

My uncle interrupted, "Jalus, you said you were not coming here to start any problems."

Jalus lunged at me and grabbed my expired passport out of the back of my pants' pocket.

The passport had no use so I laughed, "Ok, Jalus, so you have my expired passport."

Jalus began walking off, "Let's see you try to leave without this!"

I went back inside and tended to Israel. We had to wait about fifteen minutes just to make sure Jalus was not still around. The last thing we wanted to happen was for him to attack me at the airport.

While I was waiting, my uncle walked back inside and handed me my expired passport. "I told him that if he didn't give it back we would call the police."

I smiled and thanked him. It was time to leave. I had forty-five minutes to get on my flight. We all jumped in the car and off we went. I had to duck the whole time so that if Jalus was nearby he would not see Israel or me. My heart raced. I just wanted to be a mom now and hold both my children in my arms. I wanted to live a non-violent life for a change. I just wanted to be safe and have my children safe. I missed Lilly and wanted to get back to her. I wanted to make up for all the time I had lost with her. As we drove to the airport I just kept thinking of every beating I had received from Jalus. I had counted forty times in four years. I didn't count the times I was just punched or a slapped. It would have been much more.

When we arrived at the airport I was nervous. I kept glancing at the entry doors to make sure Jalus wasn't going to walk through them. My uncle, aunt and their son were helping me to distract Israel so I could get our bags checked. As I handed Israel's passport to the customer service agent she paused. "Because your son is born on the island he will need a waiver to fly." Suddenly my heart dropped. I knew how long a waiver took and even if rushed it took at least a day or a couple of hours.

My aunt said, "You and my son go to the Passport Office and see if they can get it done."

As I walked outside the airport I looked up at the sky and said, "God, if you truly want me off this island and want me to leave Jalus, then make it happen."

My flight was now leaving in thirty minutes. I knew the fate of us leaving relied on God and whoever was working to allow the waiver.

As we approached the counter my cousin said, "They have a flight that leaves in twenty minutes and this little guy needs a waiver."

To my surprise, the lady working took the money my cousin gave her and handed over Israel's waiver. We now had fifteen minutes to catch my flight. My heart kept beating faster and faster as we approached the airport once again. Then we checked in and I thanked my aunt, uncle and cousin for helping us. Israel and I walked through the security. I was so happy. I texted Celest and Riz and told them how much I loved and appreciated them.

I looked over and saw Jalus' cousin staring at Israel and I. I wasn't worried though. By the time he would text Jalus and tell him that we were at the airport we would already be on the plane.

Riz texted me and I will never forget it. She told me how proud she was of me and how beautiful of a person I was. She said she loved me as a friend and that I deserved so much better. It touched my heart and soul that my friends were proud of me.

Then I heard my flight called to start boarding. I could feel my flesh telling me to not get on the plane, but I kept asking God to guard my heart and mind. I forced myself to board the plane. I didn't know what I was going to do with my life, but I knew that it was in God's hands. As the plane took off I looked at the island below me. The island that held so many bad memories would remain, and for once in my life, I was choosing to leave them behind for good. I began to hear God talk to me on the plane.

He said, "Share what you just went through with the man next to you." So I did. I somehow felt empowered now. Then I heard God say, "When you get to California, value your children and your family and enjoy life."

Chapter Ten

"You are valuable because you exist. Not because of what you do or what you have done, but simply because you are."

–Max Lucado

It seemed like it took forever, but Israel and I finally arrived in California and my dad was there to meet us at the airport. I hugged him so tightly when I saw him. *Now this is love, to feel safe and not feel like I am going to be harmed.* That night I fell into a deep sleep. It was so peaceful knowing that I could actually sleep in safely and know that no one was going to hurt me.

When I awoke the next morning something was wrong. I went to get out of bed and I could barely walk across the floor. I felt out of breath and dizzy. All the pain I felt a week ago when I got beat up came back one hundred times worse.

My parents saw me and said, "You need to be taken to the hospital." My mother was concerned because I still had a lump in my cheekbone. One of my pupils was very dilated as well. When we arrived at the hospital I knew something was wrong. I remembered what the doctor had said at the hospital on the island, but I was not allowed to stay. Of course, I didn't get my results down there so I was in fear now to find out what damage had actually been done.

My mom walked me into the hospital and I was admitted and sent immediately to get a CT scan. As we waited for the results my mom said, "I hope you are ok, Love."

Then the doctor walked in. "To begin with, you have a severe concussion. You also have a totally broken sinus cavity and possibly some cracked ribs."

My mom's jaw dropped and her face turned full of anger. She just started shaking with rage. I was enraged as well just knowing that Jalus had done this to me. The thought that I had married such an evil person was overwhelming. I was confused, though, about how I had not felt this much pain until now. So I asked the doctor. He explained that my body went into shock and my adrenaline from being so afraid is what possibly stopped my body from crashing.

After we left the hospital and filed a police report on Jalus, we arrived back at the house. I was given heavy pain medication to keep my body calm and to help me heal. I was just standing in my kitchen when God began talking to me, giving me words and answers I have never known before in my life. Then God said, "Write."

Now I know you must be thinking what happens to the happy ending of the story. Well, sometimes the end of a story is just a beginning of another.

Epilogue

The conversation

These words were given to me by God the day I began writing this book.

Do not let any man or woman consume you that you forget your true calling.

Do not look for love in your flesh, no bars and drinking, and expect it to work out.

The flesh will choke your spirit and what God has planned for you.

Do not let anyone make you feel like your past has demeaned you and taken your future. You are changed by Christ.

Do not expect to find true, pure love if God is not the main focus for God is love.

Do not let Satan distract you with these people. You may just be the stepping-stone to show them God is love. If they choose not to change then leave. Christ was the living sacrifice not you.

Do not lose your relationship with God trying to save someone who is not ready to change.

I cried to God, "Why me?"

He responded, "You had to show them My love, My forgiveness and My grace. Your suffering was not in vain."

God said to me, "When I cut him off, you didn't listen. I wasn't done talking."

Do not become bitter and angry—it will make you lose focus.

By the time you finish writing this book, everything will make sense and you will be happier than you have been in your entire life.

Satan will try to stop you from writing your story.

I cried to God, "Why is it so hard to write all this stuff that happened to me?"

He responded, "You never forgave yourself for all of it. You let people you dated condemn you for it. Forgive yourself. I love you."

Don't ever let Satan tell you, you can't have a great life and you messed everything up. It's a lie to keep you in bondage so you stay distracted from what God has planned for you.

The more battles you have been through in your life and the hard situations you've been through is because you have a big calling on your life. If you have been through hell it's because God has a big calling for you to help people defeat their hell.

When you have that feeling that says, "Don't go" then don't! It could be that your very life is on the line. Rest and let God talk.

We are all afraid to say, "God have Your will," but God wants to give us the desires of our heart. He will make you happy.

Never let anything or anyone become so important to you that you cannot live without it and let it become more important in your life than God. Satan sets people up like this to lose focus on God. Then they become so broken without these people or things. Satan will use people and things to kill you, or destroy you and cancel the calling God has for you.

God cannot force someone to change. It is a choice. It's a choice to let go of your past and to forgive others. It's a choice not to judge because God gave us grace.

Have you trusted in God even half as much as you have trusted in people, or even yourself?

Some of us are all in bondage. Maybe in bondage to jobs, money, sickness, disease or material sex. Put God first for two weeks. Say every time these things seem to control you and make your mind wonder, "God, guard my heart and my mind" and you will be released from your bondage. God will show you your true calling. It's your choice.

You have trusted in everyone and everything, but do this and I will prove you wrong.

www.ingramcontent.com/pod-product-compliance
Lightning Source LLC
Chambersburg PA
CBHW070108120526
44588CB00032B/1386